What a wonderful book this is! As ~~...~~
spiritual practices and participating in life-changing holistic ~~manual therapy~~
*from John F. Barnes myofascial release helped her to peel the dense layers that
hid the beauty of her inner soul. Her writing stands out as well crafted,
meaningful, authentic and gripping in detail as she paints the pictures of
her life of crisis during The Troubles in Northern Ireland as a child. She
describes her own journey in healing as an adult, and then gives meaningful
suggestions to the reader of how we also can work toward letting love reach
where it never was before. I recommend this book wholeheartedly.*

~Carol M Davis, DPT, EdD, MS, FAPTA
JF Barnes Myofascial Release Physical Therapist
Professor Emerita, Department of Physical Therapy
University of Miami Miller School of Medicine

*From the terrorist bomb attacks of her childhood in Northern Ireland to
her lifelong battle for self-discovery, Julie McCammon reveals the snapshots
of her pathway in this personal Memoir. Traumas are inevitable, and if
we have the courage to look, the wounds can open many pathways into our
personal and collective freedom. In a beautiful way, we are not called to do
this journey alone. In the hands of another human, Julie began her journey
into freedom through Myofascial Release Therapy. As she moves from patient
to practitioner through this healing art, she serves as the light in both places.
Julie's path is her own, but the arc of her journey is one that we all must take.
In the end, you are the master and the healer that you are seeking to find,
but don't try to get there alone.*

~Zach Bush MD, Internal Medicine,
Endocrinology and Metabolism,
Hospice and Palliative Care

This book teaches us how to have a conversation with our body and soul as Julie's 'feeling intelligence' shines in this beautiful journey. After reading, many will find a way to disable a bomb from their past and learn how to rewrite a story; a new, true story of their very own. Healing is not only messy and wavy but also possible to be voiced on paper.

~Peter Podbielski, PT, MFR Therapist, Arizona

This book felt like it was written for me, asking me to show up, to start living a congruent life that is full of integrity. For me, this book has given me permission to listen, to love, to speak my truth, to share my story and to know that I am worthy.

I feel seen by her and her story. So much of what she writes resonates with me, with my heart. My body has started to talk to me or maybe this book has allowed me to start to listen. I felt like the author was writing me home. Now I am encouraged to write my own story and to speak my own words.

~Tanya Barber, Coach, Canada.

This is a courageous and hopeful book. With honesty and integrity, we are drawn into Julie's journey and, at the same time, given very helpful insights into the gift of Myofascial Release Therapy.

~Rev. Dr. Ruth Patterson, BA, BD, MSW, Northern Ireland

Whether you are currently suffering from trauma, in chronic pain seeking relief, or you are a therapist or practitioner in the healing arts, this book is for you! Beautifully written and with great vulnerability, Julie gently guides us through her own personal healing journey. An empowering and heartfelt expression of healing and transformation that demonstrates the power of what is possible. A true gift of love!

~Deborah Epstein, LMT, MFR Therapist,
Spiritual Creativity Guide, Sedona

As a therapist, I am always hoping that people will discover what they need in order to move forward. In this powerfully honest book, Julie McCammon shares with her readers lessons from her own lifelong journey towards that discovery. Personal, yet achingly universal, this book is for healers... as well as for those hoping to heal.

~Danny Carragher, PhD, Clinical Psychologist, New York

Myofascial Release (MFR) is described as a hands-on manual therapy used as part of a rehabilitation programme for the treatment of persistent pain.

However, despite this accurate clinical description, it fails to describe the true essence of the work which immerses the receiver in a profound and enlightening journey of discovery, something Julie experienced first-hand. Julie's experiences during and after her MFR training resulted in her writing this beautiful, inspiring and honest account of her travels as she says, 'learning to listen to my soul'.

As Julie so eloquently puts it, 'our bodies are continually crying out for our gaze to turn inward' and 'our soul is pleading for us to stop running and arrive'. It takes skilled, nurturing and patient hands, like Julie's, to be with you on your journey of discovery, never forcing but instead, being with and supporting you as you break through barrier after barrier of unresolved physical and emotional bracing patterns to, as Julie describes it, 'discover the diamond within'.

~Ruth Duncan, Vice-chair -
Scottish Massage Therapists Organisation(SMTO)
Executive committee (MFR) -
Association of Physical and Natural Therapists (APNT)
Director - Myofascial Release UK (MFR UK)
Author of 'A Hands-on Guide to Myofascial Release', Scotland

FINDING *mystery* WITHIN

A life-changing journey of healing and hope through the power of listening to your own body.

julie mccammon

Copyright 2021 ©Julie McCammon

All rights reserved. No part of this book may be reproduced or transmitted in any form or by any means, electronic or mechanical, including photocopying, recording, or by any information storage and retrieval system without written permission of the publisher, except for the inclusion of brief quotations in a review.

Illustrations and Cover Design by Lara Czornyj

Paperback ISBN: 978-0-578-94341-1

Dedication

To Jacob and Sophie.
Thank you for the constant reminder
to follow my dreams –
as you both lead by example, and for bringing
a beautiful blend of the science of medicine
and the healing art of music into our lives.

Contents

Part One

Part Two

Foreword

BY JOHN F. BARNES

I've had the pleasure of knowing Julie McCammon, PT, for a number of years. Julie is from Ireland and has taken a multitude of my Myofascial Release seminars. She is a highly experienced physiotherapist and an expert level Myofascial Release therapist. Her book has a message for you if you're struggling with pain, health issues or want to take your life to a higher level of joy and true health. Although her story is unique, it will resonate with many of you since we've all gone through many struggles in our lives. Julie provides you with hope and is a very good, articulate writer and a very determined, strong woman whom I greatly admire.

What many don't realize is that the theory behind healthcare is logical but terribly flawed and incomplete. This theory has completely eliminated the mind and has an erroneous understanding of the fascial system. Traditional healthcare views us as mindless machines and/or bags of chemicals. This fragmentation of the human being started over 300 years ago where the father of modern medicine, Renee Descartes, Isaac Newton and a number of other scientists had gotten into a fight with the church. Descartes wanted cadavers to be able to study anatomy and the church would have none of it. I think what eventually happened is they all kind of gave up and they fragmented the human being. The church got the spirit, physicians got the biochemistry, therapists got the flesh and nobody wanted the emotions. Today, this fragmentation has reached the point of absurdity!

Julie will be sharing with you her experiences with Myofascial Release. When I went to Physical Therapy school, during anatomy class, as we dissected cadavers, we were told by the professor to cut away the fascia because it's totally unimportant packing material. My experience of over 60 years as a Physical Therapist, treating people from all over the world, has shown me that fascia is one of the most important structures in our body. Its fluid component, which is called the ground substance, has been ignored. Our consciousness flows through the fluidity of the fascial system. All the nutrition we ingest, the air we breathe, the fluid we drink, the biochemistry, hormones, energy and information that every cell needs to thrive must go through the fluidity of the fascial system in order for the trillions of our cells to thrive.

All research has been done on dead people and as you know, dead people are brittle and have no consciousness. Sadly, this is the model of reality of the human being we were taught as healthcare professionals. There are a couple of other very big problems. Physical and/or emotional trauma, surgery, and thwarted inflammatory processes can solidify the fluidity of the fascial system. The ground substance becomes more and more viscous overtime and hardens into crushing pressure on pain sensitive structures that produce the symptoms that you may have been experiencing. Fascial restrictions can generate a tensile strength of up to 2,000 lbs per square inch of pressure. Unfortunately, these restrictions don't show up on any of the standard testing that you may have had, so it's been misdiagnosed for eons.

The good news is Myofascial Release is safe, highly effective at reducing pain, tightness and restoring our physiological health. Because we do have a mind, there is something missed in traditional healthcare that I call subconscious protective patterns. A lot of copycat courses have risen since I started teaching Myofascial Release some 50 years ago. The problem is they are teaching what I call the old form of Myofascial Release which forces a system that can't be forced, producing only temporary results.

Authentic Myofascial Release is gentle, never injures and provides the hope that you can restore your health, your function, eliminate pain and find your true self.

I hope you enjoy Julie's wonderful book.

John F. Barnes, PT

Myofascial Release Treatment Centers and Seminars

800-327-2425

www.MyofascialRelease.com

Malvern@myofascialrelease.com

Introduction

WE ARE ALL MADE OF STORY

Who is to say that maybe your greatest calling is not to pass on the stories and lessons of your ordinary life?

We are all travelling along our own path on this journey called life. We might not be walking side by side, I may be a few steps behind you. But this is my story and where I have found myself along the way.

Whether we know it or not, we are constantly telling a story with our lives, through our actions, our conversations and even in our silences.

At the heart of every story is transformation, or the belief in the possibility of change.

My hope is that by writing my own story, it will not only help others on their journey of healing and growing, but that it will also help me to unravel who I am and who I truly want to become.

We all have an inner story constantly evolving. It is influenced by those around us, by their words, cruel or kind, and by our choices, good or bad.

'We are pattern makers -

and if our patterns are beautiful

and full of grace, they will

be able to bring a person

for whom the world has become

broken and disorganised

up off his knees and back to life.'

~Barry Lopez[1]

Our inner story runs deep, influencing the direction we choose. All too often, the story we tell ourselves can hinder us and hold us back.

I've come to understand that the path I walk is not simply a means to get to my destination, but it's the journey itself that has so much to offer.

I cherish my life with all its ups and downs. All of it has made me who I am today. Now in my 50s, I feel a hunger to keep learning, growing and changing. I want to be stretched. I don't want to remain stuck in a rut of comfort and ease. I wish I had developed this desire for discovery at a much younger age, but I guess I'm living proof that it is never too late.

I am learning how important it is to stop sometimes, to sit, to be still and pay attention. To open my eyes, to open my ears, to experience life with all my senses, to reach out and touch life, to make contact with myself, to engage and interact on a deeper level with what lies beneath my skin, reconnecting with my soul. Deep inside, there is a voice, with its own story, but we never stop to listen. Instead, we walk, we run, we race through life, focused on what pushes and pulls us from the outside.

Our soul is trying to tell us something that our heart and our body don't yet know.

We tend to look only at the broad brushstrokes rather than our very own detailed inner landscape that is crying out for attention. We choose to ignore the intricate web of golden threads inside. We look without seeing or hearing - without truly listening.

During my journey, I have come to learn that we have all the information we need right inside of us. However, we all get caught up with what's going on around us, forgetting the beauty that lies within.

My deepest desire is to be medicine for someone else's pain by sharing my journey. It is a journey that has required surrendering to my own soul, allowing myself to be swallowed whole.

As I take you along on my journey of discovery, I want you to know that I don't have it all worked out. I don't have all the answers, far from it! In fact, I regularly have one of those days that drain away every ounce of clarity I thought I had gained. But I know deep down that everyone deserves to heal and find joy after the storm. So I choose to remain open to growing, learning and evolving. I hope you enjoy this collection of lessons, inspirations and stories from my own journey. A journey that has brought me to discover myself as a deeper mystery.

As I have travelled new paths, it has enabled me to bring myself home into my body, to the seat of my heart, where my soul resides. It's here where I feel at home in my own skin, where I now feel full of purpose, more engaged and more alive than ever before. I feel a newfound sense of belonging deep in the marrow of my bones.

I'm learning to trust my own voice, my own unique expression and to actually believe it will bring healing to others. I am trusting it will bring joy and it will bring hope as I let go and let it flow onto every page.

I am daring to feel the power of my dreams, compelled to write, even though I have not the slightest clue where to begin or how to write a book. But somehow I can see and feel there is something magical in the process. I feel it is a risk necessary to live in alignment with my soul's calling.

For me, the process of writing and re-reading through my journals from the last 5 years, has felt like I am somehow gaining wisdom by reflecting on my life, knowing for certain that I want to share my story. As I open my heart to you, my prayer is that you will see it as an expression of my truth; that you will catch glimpses of the magic and mystery of my ordinary life, as you follow the threads of my story, woven into each and every page of this book.

'I would love to live

Like a river flows,

Carried by the surprise

Of its own unfolding.'

~John O'Donohue[2]

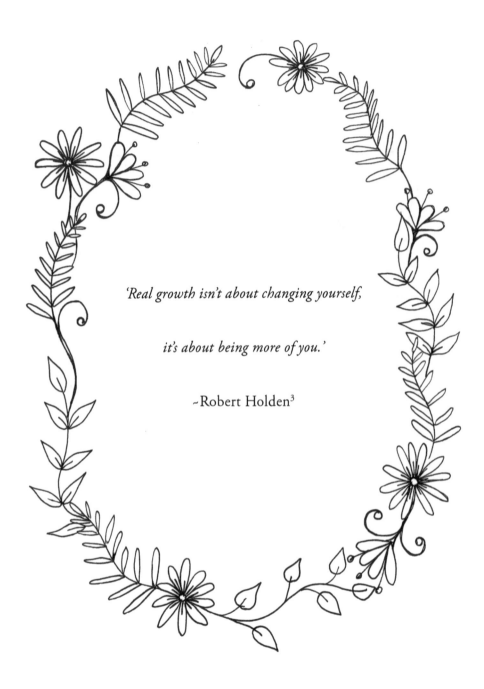

'Real growth isn't about changing yourself,

it's about being more of you.'

~Robert Holden[3]

Part One

CHAPTER ONE

Good Versus Truth

RE-STORYING

From a very young age, I knew I wanted to help others. I guess this is where I naively thought I would find some degree of self-worth. I initially wanted to be a nurse. Later on, opting for Physiotherapy, I hoped to help people walk again, ease their pain and help them return to a meaningful life following various illnesses and accidents.

I graduated as a Physiotherapist in 1990 and started working for the NHS (National Health Service). This involved working in many different settings, such as orthopedics, spinal injuries, limb fitting and rehabilitation for patients with neurological injuries or illnesses.

I loved my work, despite nearly every day coming into contact with someone who had been injured directly as a result of The Troubles. For example, one person was injured by a stray bullet severing his spinal cord, sadly being in the wrong place at the wrong time. Another tragically lost both her legs when her car was booby-trapped after she was mistakenly identified as a target. Others who were knee-capped as punishment for some unknown crime, the list could go on and on.

I remained working for the NHS until 1997 when I was then given the opportunity to work specifically in a musculoskeletal field while working as a civilian Physiotherapist for the Ministry of Defence. This involved treating mostly soldiers who were injured on duty or in training.

This was a new post that I was responsible for setting up and I enjoyed the challenge. The downside, however, was that I had to check under my car each morning before my commute to work.

Finally, I moved away from being employed and opened up my own private practice in 2004. This was my biggest challenge but also what I had always dreamed of doing and it grew from strength to strength.

Little did I know that this path would eventually lead me to study Myofascial Release (MFR) and, in doing so, I would kick a pebble that would transform not only my own body, but my mind, my emotions and my soul. I had no idea that this work would show me my actual self-worth in a totally new way.

Only now do I feel more comfortable in my own skin after years of self-loathing and beating myself up. Only now do I feel part of something bigger, part of something beautiful. Only now do I realise how much energy I've wasted by pushing myself to fit into the stories of who I thought I was supposed to be. Stories that Society said I had to live to be ok in this world. Only now do I see that I am not the story my culture made of me.

It's never too late to say no, even if I've been saying yes all of my life. It's time to emerge from where I've been hiding. Maybe it's time to write my own story, or at least one that has a different ending.

Perhaps the best place to start is not at the beginning but somewhere in the middle. The scene is a large conference room in a hotel in Cincinnati. I am there along with 150 other students, all of us about to embark on 11 days of training in something called Myofascial Release (MFR).

At this point, I had been working as a physiotherapist for about 25 years and I still got excited when learning something new. I was focused on perfecting each of the treatment techniques that would be demonstrated and taught in this course. I was looking forward to returning home to Northern Ireland with new tools to help treat my patients. All I really knew about this treatment method was that it worked with the fascia in the body. Fascia is the strong connective tissue that goes throughout the entire body, layer upon layer, surrounding everything from the organs and muscles right down to the cells that make up every part of your body. I had been told during my university training that fascia was just a bit of packaging, pretty unimportant really.

As the course started, there was a lot of talk about fascia and how to release the restrictions found in the body - it was fascinating. Then they started to talk about also releasing emotions, traumas and memories as well. I remember sitting there thinking, 'but, what do I need to release?'

'What did I need to let go off?' I tried to focus on just learning the structural releases being taught. But as we began to practice the techniques on each other, I started to feel sensations, an awareness of something going on inside my body. Where once I believed healing took place when a specific technique was applied to the body with precision, now I understood healing as a journey that takes us out of our heads and into our bodies, as we begin to weave ourselves back into the shimmering web of life that is our fascial system. It felt like my traditional physiotherapy training was good, but this MFR training was revealing a deeper layer of truth.

For me, this was a total dismantling of everything I thought I knew for certain. Little did I know that this course would not only transform how I worked as a physiotherapist, but that it would change me from the inside out and blow my mind all at the same time.

Who was I kidding, thinking I had nothing to let go of?

MEMORIES, PEOPLE, PLACES

I grew up in Northern Ireland in a small border village, just on the north side of the line that divides Ireland and so many of the people who live on this Emerald Isle. My early childhood memories are few and far between. I do, however, remember playing in my grandparents' garden where my grandfather grew his own tomatoes and grapes in a beautiful wooden greenhouse. I have never tasted fruit anywhere in the world that was as tasty as those huge purple grapes hanging on the vines in his greenhouse. The taste, the smell, the colour, are all embedded in my memory.

I remember Grandpa showing me a shot put ring he had built at the bottom of his garden for a neighbour's daughter called Mary Peters. He had built this with his own hands to enable Mary to follow her dreams and practice a sport which she loved. Little did I know or understand then the pride that he felt when she went on to win the gold medal in the 1972 Olympics in Munich, competing in the pentathlon.

I remember every Saturday morning my sister and I were allowed 10 pence worth of sweets from my parents' grocery store. 10p bought a handsome stash of sugary treats that would last us the rest of the day and sometimes well into the next day too.

And then, there were the not-so-nice memories…

We lived above our family grocery store in the main street of the village.

I remember having a vivid imagination, involving monsters and creatures, some of whom wore balaclavas as they roamed through the aisles of our shop at night. I used to hate it when mum was making dinner, only to realise she had run out of some vital ingredient. She would ask me to go down to the shop to get it for her. My heart would be pounding out of my chest as I crept into the darkness, the only light coming from the refrigeration units along with the hum of the machines keeping fresh food cold. I often held my breath and made a run for it as I listened for intruders, while being deafened by the sound of my own heart thudding inside my ears.

As a kid growing up during the height of The Troubles in Northern Ireland, fear was at the core of my very being. Day after day was filled with stories of terror and death, which my parents tried to shield me from but inevitably would find their way to my ears. Acts of terrorism were a daily occurrence, not just causing physical trauma but emotional and spiritual trauma as well. This violence against one was violence against us all.

The following scene is not only vividly etched into my mind but also woven into my body. The setting is in our little border village in Northern Ireland in the 1970s. I was about 9 years old.

It was a Friday evening and I had just returned home from fetching some fish and chips from the local chippy for everyone's dinner. As I climbed the stairs from our front door and entered the kitchen, my mouth was watering from the smell of salt and vinegar on the hot chips as it steamed through the brown paper bag.

As the kitchen door swung closed behind me, I heard shattering glass crashing to the floor, followed by a moment of complete silence where no one moved. It was like we were caught in the eye of a hurricane. Then there was a huge boom as the explosion reverberated through our home and our bodies. I will never forget dad diving for cover from the chair he was sitting in right at the front of the house. As the glass from the windows flew in around him. We all followed suit, diving for cover, stuck in the grip of fear.

We had been targeted by the IRA simply because we had served members of the police in our store. The bomb had been placed in a bin right outside our front door, the front door I had walked through just moments before.

Little did I know at the time that this fear and terror would thread its way through my body, my voice and every part of me. Indeed, fear became something so familiar to me, I barely knew it was there. It would cause me to keep myself small and silent. This was where I felt safest. I would become stuck in this cycle of staying small and fitting in for most of my life.

Even as an adult, I still gravitate towards this familiar place of safety by choosing to fade into the background. Fear creates a thread that every decision and experience in life is woven around. And from a very early age, that thread was knitted into every cell in my body.

I chose to avoid trouble by keeping my head down, fitting in, being good, and toeing the line. This came at a cost, however, as it squashed my creativity and imagination. My individuality stamped out. So, instead of feeling free to explore who I was, I did exactly what was expected of me: I chose to be good.

This pattern of behavior would go into overdrive in my early teens, as I tried to cope with rejection and the fear of being alone. It is only now that I am learning I have a choice to either speak my truth, or to just fit in and be good. For so long, good was my go-to, but this being good has held me back. It has hidden my wings and kept me silent. I am hoping that by speaking my truth, it will teach me to be brave and give me permission and space for my story to unfold.

So, as I begin to journal my thoughts and my dreams, it appears to me that there is something more than just journaling here. When it is just me and my journal, it feels like my safe place. But if I want to choose truth over good, perhaps it's time to stretch myself and write a book. I say it out loud, 'I am writing a book!'

And so I begin, little by little, to write. This writing has become my story. A story of transformation and growth. My dream is that it will somehow become that for you as well.

CHILDLIKE IMAGINATION

I remember as a child how much I loved fairy tales. I loved to escape inside each story, vividly picturing each scene, as if I was literally living in the story. I would fall asleep most nights playing scenes over and over in my head. These scenes often became my dreams.

I felt a strange sense of connection with the characters, sometimes even more so than the people I actually knew in the real world.

I found friends more easily in these stories before I found them in the world around me. Perhaps it was because I could create the happy ending I most desired in my imagination. I was in control, whereas in the real world, there was no control of the bombings and shootings in our country at that time.

I would be captivated, living and reliving every detail of the story over and over in my mind. Fully absorbed in each moment. It was as if I had discovered a door into another world, a world where I was safe.

Similarly, I would repeat the same storyline when play-acting with my older sister and her friend. It always involved me being needy for safety and security. These recurrent stories that played out in my imagination, became a way that I could escape, leaving a trail of breadcrumbs so that someone could find me and rescue me from the snares and traps in the dark wood.

As I grew up, I realised I had to learn how to rescue myself.

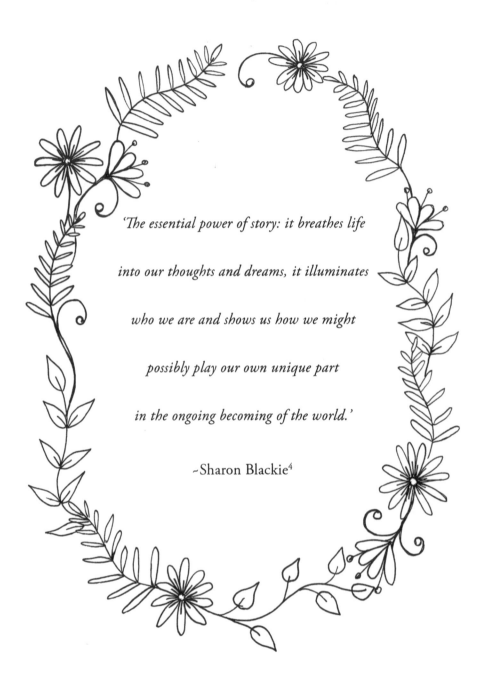

'The essential power of story: it breathes life

into our thoughts and dreams, it illuminates

who we are and shows us how we might

possibly play our own unique part

in the ongoing becoming of the world.'

~Sharon Blackie[4]

CHAPTER TWO

Life

FRACTURED

I grew up in a loving home, with everything I could ever want, a beautiful house, dogs, ponies, gardens and beauty all around. My parents both worked incredibly hard, Dad excelling in entrepreneurial business ventures, while mum worked tirelessly behind the scenes helping in every way possible. Then suddenly, at the age of 14, my world was shattered. My dad had an affair and left us.

The day he walked out through our front door will forever be etched on my mind. I desperately wanted life to continue the way it was, before the overheard conversations, before the realisation that life would never be the same again. How could my life suddenly feel so broken?

I could barely breathe. I felt eerily alone inside my own experience.

This loss gutted me and left a huge crater inside, within which an ache would grow and follow me to this day. This ache is a longing to belong.

The place inside my body where abandonment carved out its hole, felt dark, damp and cold.

I tried so hard to not feel the pain, I shoved it down so deep, all I felt was numb. As hard as I tried to forget Dad, I could not. He was everywhere; in everything and everyone.

When Dad left, my heart broke for my Mum, as I watched her world come tumbling down around her. How she coped was to retreat into her bedroom and take sleeping tablets to try to numb her pain. I somehow felt it was my mission to comfort her and try to put her back together. I needed her, as my sister was soon to head off to University in Scotland, so it would just be me and Mum. Looking back now, all three of us retreated into our bedrooms a lot. I guess we were all trying to escape the reality of what was happening in the real world.

It was so hard to watch my mum's heart being broken and denied. Everything had happened so suddenly - we were all in shock and felt completely numb, not knowing how to do life without Dad. Each layer of numbness was protecting our hearts from shattering. Mum somehow developed a fierce self-reliance that still, to this day, makes it difficult for her to reach out and ask for help. This independence was necessary to enable her to cope on her own.

Trauma like this sometimes makes it more difficult for our hurting and broken heart to remember that we have hidden gems inside. We can lose sight of who we were created to be as the overwhelming emptiness takes centre stage.

During this time, I too slipped into a darkness, listening to the voices inside my head which were on repeat, voices that told me I hated myself, that I was ugly, I was useless, that I would never be enough. I spent so much time and energy pushing my sadness back inside my body, wanting to disappear, feeling that being seen or taking up space in the world was some sort of crime. I was told to not tell anyone what was going on, and this need to keep so much secret was where shame took root. So I locked everything in and everyone out. Deep down, I began to believe that there wasn't a place for me in this world. I felt like an outsider.

As I clawed my way through life, I also learned self-reliance. I believed I was the only thing on the planet that could be counted on. This huge burden was crushing me under its weight and my only escape to safety was to lock myself away inside my own head. Maybe this is why I have always felt so alone, why I have struggled to find a sense of belonging. No wonder I always held myself back, tending to keep things on a surface level, often afraid to go deeper, afraid of what I might find.

In the months that followed, I had not only lost my dad but we had also lost our home. For lots of different reasons, we had to move out of our seven-bedroom house in the country, with stables and a tennis court and into a caravan for a year.

I can honestly say that this was the worst year of my life. It was a particularly cold winter and I remember one freezing morning when I poured boiling water out of the kettle into a mug to make some tea, the mug shattered into pieces, as it had been so cold even inside the caravan. As I stared at the shattered mug on the countertop, it looked and felt like my fractured life.

Eventually, I began to search for worth and tried desperately to prove my value, not to my mum, for I knew that she loved me and accepted me, but to everyone else around me. I quickly fell into the trap of trying to prove myself. Striving to achieve, to succeed, never sitting still, never stopping long enough to count my blessings. I was continually aiming higher. I started to feel that in order to be fully human, I must want to progress. It was one of my defining characteristics. I was listening to a definitive and unassailable explanation of how life should be. I became trapped inside this story and it had become so much a part of me that I scarcely noticed it. My only goals in life were to be a good respectable girl, with a great career. This intense sense of personal ambition festered inside me. The constant striving for success and recognition seemed somehow normal.

I was totally blind to the beauty of my beingness. I couldn't even begin to grasp that I was already abundant and beautiful. Part of me still longed to feel worthy deep in my bones. But other parts of me were deeply tired from all the searching for the gifts I already possess, but just couldn't see.

My scatteredness prevented me from stopping and breathing long enough to hear the rumblings within. As the shock wore off and the numbness began to dissolve, I felt responsible for getting Mum through this, trying to be the perfect daughter, being good and working hard. The more I tried, however, the more alone I found myself. This self-reliant lifestyle was lonely, but I was stuck and couldn't see any other way to survive. So I forged ahead as a lone wolf, remaining trapped in this place of disconnection for years to come.

I began to internalise the pain and the rejection, and this is undoubtedly where I started to travel down the path of self-hatred. I guess also watching Mum display a total disregard for herself didn't help either.

The years that followed were some of the darkest of my life. Where I grew into unbelonging. I felt fractured, split open, raw and ashamed.

Only now looking back, I can see it was necessary for me to stand in my unbelonging in order to eventually find my way home. Trying, failing and learning is, after all, how we grow.

POST VIRAL FATIGUE

All my striving had accomplished something, as I graduated with an Honours Degree in Physiotherapy in 1990. I loved my work and enjoyed helping my patients gain relief from their pain and improve their function and independence. I was also happily married to Peter, whom I had known since I was about the age of 12.

I had first met Peter when we were both in the same Sunday school class and we started dating when I was 17. Eight years later, we got married and not long after that, we welcomed our children, Jacob and Sophie. Our family life was full and working as a Physiotherapist meant things were busy, but still, something wasn't quite enough on the achievement front for me. So when the possibility arose for me to travel to Nepal to do some teaching, I jumped at the opportunity.

Off I went to visit friends who were working in a hospital in Amppipal, somewhere in the foothills of the Himalayas. I made the journey on my own to Kathmandu and then was accompanied by my friends out to the remote hospital. This journey is definitely the kind of journey you will never forget.

We had two long bus rides out of the city. It was roughly 6 hours by bus, from Kathmandu to Dumre and then Dumre to Turture. Each bus was crowded with people and animals and all kinds of other luggage, both inside and every available inch outside; anywhere someone could cling to or where something could be strapped down. The smells, the sounds and the colours were causing sensory overload.

The last 6 hours of the journey were on foot. We climbed along narrow paths cut into the hillside with sheer drops off the side. The views were stunning, like nothing I had ever seen before. There were rice fields cut into the landscape - everything was so green. There was no sound of traffic as there were no roads for miles, just well-trodden paths cutting their way up the mountainsides. The silence was beautiful, with only the distant sounds of children's voices as they played or carried heavy jugs of water to their homes. The porters carried my luggage and other supplies for the hospital up the hills, chatting away in Nepali.

I spent the first few days recovering from the journey. Then, I jumped straight into teaching some of the hospital staff how to perform basic physiotherapy skills, as there was no physiotherapy offered to the patients at present. I loved passing on these simple teachings and techniques that I thought might be of help. All of the staff members I worked alongside were so lovely and with the aid of a translator, I taught the nursing staff how to safely mobilise their patients following surgery and how to do some basic Respiratory Physiotherapy with those who had chest conditions. All was going great and I was really enjoying the experience.

Then a blinding headache came out of nowhere and I entered a state of delirium for the next 4 or 5 days. All of my strength abandoned me. I became so ill I thought I would never see my family again, I would never make it home. I couldn't keep any water down. Luckily, I was staying in the home of my friends who worked as a doctor and a nurse at the hospital. They put up a drip to keep me hydrated and nursed me in their own home.

As the time approached for my return flights, we all knew I had to somehow get back down to Kathmandu. But I still couldn't even lift my head off the pillow without being violently sick. My head was pounding as if someone was literally bouncing up and down with their feet on my head. We talked through the possible options.

First of all, we could get two porters to carry me down the six-hour descent in a hammock suspended on a pole between them- those poor souls! This did not feel like a viable option as I really didn't think I'd make it.

The second option, and the only other way out of those foothills, was by helicopter. I'd never been in one before, but this felt like a safer option. The day came and they marked out a large white X with toilet-roll on the only flat bit of ground up the hillside from where we were living. This marked the spot where the helicopter would land. It arrived safely, much to the amusement of all the local villagers. My friend David, who was the doctor, and I climbed into the backseat of the helicopter. Much to my horror, the two boys flying this contraption looked around 18 years old or younger. One was resting the instruction manual on his knee. Obviously, I was not full of confidence that I would even make it to Kathmandu, never mind Ireland.

Arriving in Kathmandu, I was immediately taken to the hospital. It was here they decided to do a lumbar puncture (spinal tap), in order to drain some cerebro-spinal fluid, so that they could run tests to confirm what they suspected, which was that I had viral meningitis.

The journey home was horrendous. I flew within 24-hours of having a lumbar puncture, something I would strongly recommend not to do! Unfortunately, my medical insurance would not let me fly home unless I had a diagnosis, and so this procedure was necessary. My head literally felt like it was going to explode the entire flight back to London.

When I landed in London, thankfully my husband Peter was there to meet me. As soon as I saw him, I collapsed, having just got off the worst flight of my life. I was taken by ambulance to a local hospital. The doctors there wanted to do another lumbar puncture as they were hesitant to trust the results from a developing country. I just remember telling Peter under no circumstances to give them permission to do another lumbar puncture and to ask them to just give me an injection of pain relief to get me home on the next flight from London to Belfast. I made it home the next morning, but this illness had totally knocked the wind out of my sails.

Welcome to the world of post-viral fatigue. Little did I know this fatigue, brain fog, aches and pains would plague me on and off for the next 15 years until I discovered John F. Barnes Myofascial Release. Fatigue made me feel like something or someone had stolen me from my own body. My body was still here visible to those around me, but it felt like I wasn't really in it. Something had sucked me out of myself. Everything was hazy and numb, as if there was a missing scene from my life, as I slowly faded into nothingness. Life felt like it held no vibrant colours, just shades of grey. It felt like when you go to bed really late and then get up ridiculously early with no coffee in sight. Only you feel like this 24/7.

My legs felt like they were sinking into quicksand even with a simple task like trying to walk up the stairs. Every ounce of energy was being sucked out of my body and my limbs were feeling impossibly heavy. My head was so thick with fog, I found it impossible to concentrate or think clearly.

This constant feeling of being somewhere behind my own body, unable to catch up, forgetting what it felt like to actually be inside my own body, caused me to withdraw from social events. Instead, I was buried under a thick mist somewhere in the corner of the room, watching from afar. As well as the constant battle with fatigue, there was constant pain. My muscles ached, my joints were sore and my head was pounding. Pain is obviously physically debilitating, but it also saps all of your energy and holds you hostage.

This struggle with post-viral fatigue caused a complete separation from my familiar healthy active lifestyle. I went from running 4-5 times a week to barely being able to walk the dogs. Once I had dragged myself through a day at work, I had nothing left to give. My work got the best of me. But as difficult as it was, this illness turned out to be the very thing that developed a curiosity and a longing to discover a truer encounter with life and with healing. Eventually, I realised it was not a problem to be fixed, and believe me I had spent years trying desperately to fix myself. But this illness itself was teaching me how to heal so much more than the symptoms it had given me.

I have to admit that sometimes the fatigue was made worse by my own relentless struggle to push on through, despite everything in my body screaming at me to slow down. After all, pushing through was what I did best. But eventually, I'd had enough. It was as if I let myself break open. Only then did I begin to understand that I needed to take time to allow the despair and darkness that lay deep inside of me to connect me back to myself. All this being caught up in pushing through had resulted in me losing who I truly was. I had lost myself. Despite the outward appearance of having it all together, I was actually collapsing with exhaustion and grief.

I was about to learn that I needed to take time to not only lick my wounds, but also to fully explore them before I could let them heal. I was being brought into a place of reunion with the life I was meant to be living. Only by going on this exact journey was I able to hear my soul calling me home.

So much of my life has been lived on the surface as opposed to diving deep inside. I had become caught up in a cycle of compulsive avoidance, an addiction to not wanting to know my darkness. Instead, trying desperately to cover it up with beautiful things, with comforting foods and with achievements. These were all things done in innocence - I didn't realise at the time what I was doing.

Post-viral fatigue brought me to breaking point, where I thought I was going to have to give up my work as a Physiotherapist. I loved my work and it defined so much of what I was at that time. Without that, I felt useless. But I would never have discovered Myofascial Release, had I not been on this journey. I would never have got the opportunity to go on this rollercoaster ride that is taking me into consciousness and to a place of true belonging.

Before this, I had to fully enter into my lostness, to discover what my darkness was trying to teach me. Myofascial Release showed me how to more fully encounter my own body. My body was so full of pain, stiffness and fatigue that I had grown accustomed to ignoring it and pushing through. This treatment began to help me see that buried deep within my heart, I had a longing. My heart was aching for me to come home. I now realise I had spent so much time outside of my body trying to avoid the pain and fatigue. Something in me longed for a coming together, a cohesion of body, mind, emotions and soul.

I began to discover that my internal landscape was always pulling me home, if only I had listened. Instead, for years I had ignored, numbed and buried this voice, this longing, so deep inside that I had no idea that it even existed. I was beginning to see, to feel and to hear that I had a place where I belonged. A place of my very own, calling to me, remembering me into belonging. This treatment started a process in me that brought liberation, forgiveness and healing, calling me into living my life in this one precious body.

CHAPTER THREE

The World Of Myofascial Release

Four months prior to my trip to America to start my MFR training and years after battling fatigue, brain fog and chronic pain, I was finally given a tentative diagnosis of Fibromyalgia from my GP. I did not readily accept this diagnosis and knew all too well how often it was misdiagnosed. So often it is used as a blanket term when people's symptoms don't fit into any other box. This was a label that I did not want.

I had found my way here to Cincinnati after years of struggling with illness. I was at the point where I thought I was going to have to stop working as a Physiotherapist. This struggle had begun to strip away my identity. I began to question what I had to offer, how could I be of value, how could I contribute, or even, was I worthy of love? My insecurities and doubts went deep. Perhaps these questions were there all along, but it was only in the deepest darkest moments that they began to emerge. I was at the point where I was struggling to even walk the dogs, never mind run

or exercise like I had been able to do for years before. After a day at work, I was fit for nothing, not even a conversation. I felt as if I was no longer lovable since I had nothing to offer in return. My heart even felt somehow anaesthetised. I felt numb.

The best way to explain what happened next was that MFR helped me to break open the walls of protection I had built around my heart and helped me to learn to make a truer encounter with life. So when John F. Barnes offered to treat me, it would have been rude not to accept. Especially after witnessing others falling over themselves to have the opportunity to experience John at work.

For me to be willing to get up on a stage in front of over 100 people, believe me, I must have felt some sort of compulsion. My heart was thumping out of my chest and my legs shaking, my mouth was dry, but somewhere deep inside I knew I had to say yes. I not only found my voice that day but, against all the odds, I actually discovered how to use it. I made my way up onto the stage, legs still shaking, but as I did so I felt a strange confidence that saying yes to this offer would unlock something mysterious inside. I would later realise that saying yes was giving me the key to unlock the mystery within.

John was calm, grounded, down to earth and fatherly. Immediately putting me at ease as he gently cradled my head in his hands, encouraging me to let go, to melt and soften. I let down some walls and my journey began.

I felt a sense of boundlessness like there were no barriers between his hands and my head, as if they were almost merging together. I felt safe, held, supported and connected.

I was to discover that MFR meets you right where you are, taking you no further than you are willing to go. It always softens you leaving you feeling more present in your own body. I felt a newfound freedom. Was this the healing I hadn't even known I was looking for? In those early days, I began to realise just how confined I felt inside my own body and how this was not a nice feeling. This treatment somehow gave me a glimpse of something new, a sense of being part of something bigger, no longer separated, solitary. Slowly my body began to change, to open, to soften, to let go and heal. For the first time ever, I started to feel at home in my own body. This treatment was not just a physical treatment of the bodily structures, it was so much more.

During one of my first experiences of MFR, when I actually allowed myself to let go and make a noise, it felt like I let myself cross a threshold of initiation. I became a witness to the pain I had held inside for too long. I became a witness to the shattering of the armour I had built. I began to find the courage to shed those layers of protection and shatter my own armour, causing my heart to be open to receiving more beauty, more love and more belonging. This was the beginning of a discovery that there was a home I'd never known waiting right inside. A place within where everything is allowed to flower in its own perfect time and way.

Let me try to explain how Myofascial Release not only addresses physical symptoms, but also releases emotions and traumas trapped inside our bodies: I want to take you on a journey of discovery showing how MFR began the process of healing my mind, body and soul.

DISCOVERING SOMETHING NEW

My post-viral fatigue/fibromyalgia, caused me to step off the path I had planned and that I was relentlessly pursuing. I knew I was unable to keep going down this particular path of treating more than 10 patients a day and running my own business. Something had to change.

When I stepped off the plane arriving in America, I also stepped off that path. I made a discovery of something new. I found a new trail, a new path that was leading to a whole new adventure of healing, a whole new way of living.

I never could have dreamed where this path would take me. This new path showed me to pay attention to my gut, to my intuition. I was no longer blindly following the path I had started out on. It felt like I was

'When our eyes see our hands

doing the work of our hearts,

the circle of Creation is completed inside us.

The doors of our souls fly open and love steps

forth to heal everything in sight.'

~Michael Bridge[5]

now walking with my eyes wide open, my ears open and my senses alert. Something worthwhile was definitely catching my attention. I gave myself permission to take this detour. It was life-changing!

I discovered that I really hadn't a clue just how amazing our bodies are. I knew only the standard textbook understanding of anatomy and physiology, a very linear knowledge. MFR shifted my whole world.

A few days into the course, I had listened to others around me scream, cry and shout, as their emotions bubbled to the surface. Everything being released into the air around us as they were encouraged to let it out.

Of course, I remained reserved and quiet, the way I had learned to live my life. I listened to the instructors say time and time again, 'trust your body's wisdom and let go', 'emotions need to be released', 'your body is trying to get rid of it for a reason'. I listened to some share how amazing the release felt and how much lighter they felt afterwards.

Then during one session that afternoon, I was lying on the treatment table while someone was practicing a release somewhere on my head.

One of the instructors walked by and placed his hand gently on my solar plexus. They often did this just to encourage you out of your head, away from your thoughts and into your body to feel and soften. As he touched me, an uncontrollable wave of emotion swept through my body. I began to cry silent tears. He lent down and told me that I needed to give a voice to this pain. His hand moved to the right and hit a spot just below my ribs that was so extremely painful that I had to make a noise. Despite thinking that the room was so silent right now, I wanted to control myself in the silence. But I felt safe, and I knew I needed to cry with the sound of my voice. I needed to stop choking or squeezing my silent tears back inside. I needed to really cry, to hear it with my heart. This was important to the journey of my soul.

As I let go and trusted my body's wisdom, I didn't even recognise the noise that came out of my throat. Along with the tears and the noise that came out that day, there was also a lot of anger, grief and loss bubbling to the surface as the dam opened. Looking back now, I understand that my body needed to scream that loud to get my attention. Afterwards, I felt liberated that I had let go of all my guarding and bracing. It felt like I had been living my life stuck down the rabbit hole, and now I had the courage to stick my nose up through the undergrowth, seeing there was a whole beautiful world out there that I'd been missing. I had been absolutely lost within myself, consumed by negative image, low self-esteem and feelings of never being enough. But now I could see a chink of light. I could see that there was more to life. A whole new world was waiting just outside the rabbit hole, and I decided to step over the threshold.

I realised that somehow I had lost my place in the world, I had hidden my stories for safekeeping and then forgotten where I had hidden them. I guess I had developed a tough skin and I was hiding somewhere underneath it. This thick skin had caused me to lose sight of myself. It had developed with threats, violence, grief and abandonment, leading me down a path without heart. I had cleverly found a way to survive by hiding myself but now I felt called to change, to wake up and to see. I was being called to take my part in the great unfolding of this life, rather than being forever lost in the wasteland of my own existence.

Often, our fascial web seems to become clogged with untruths about who we are. It's an accumulation of conditions that we have accepted, roles we have played, traumas we have endured and belief systems we have unquestioningly adopted. I was beginning to see my web was full, inflexible and weighed down with so much fear, anxiety, worry, anger, guilt and frustration. So much of my life was driven by fear and the need to prove something. Constantly attempting to feel better about myself, to feel worthy and deserving of love. Yet all this striving for worthiness never resulted in anything new. I was stuck in the toxicity of my own making.

I jumped in with both feet. I did not want to return home still carrying so much excess baggage. Baggage that I now knew I could leave behind.

As others placed their hands on me, I sank into my body and started to really let go, allowing myself to fully feel, searching for what lay underneath, giving my body permission to let go, tapping into an emotion, a belief, an awareness that I needed to feel so that the restrictions could be released and healing could occur at a deeper level. It was important to know that I didn't have to work it all out. In fact, the less thinking I did, the better, as I was encouraged into every sensation that arose inside my body. Sometimes I felt shaking, trembling, emotions and other sensations like twitching, pulling or unraveling. I was feeling my whole body connection and my mind-body connection, I was hearing my fascial system speak to me. I began listening to my fascial voice and let my body unwind.

I was learning how to:

Feel

Heal

Have fun

Let go

Find my voice

Laugh

Cry

Scream

Unwind

Be me

Express myself

Stretch

Find my limits

Push beyond

Walk to the edge

Jump

Fly.

FULL DISCLOSURE

I have to admit that when I arrived in America for my very first taste of MFR, I think I was suffering from a bit of culture shock. These Americans were loud! Their emotions came flooding to the surface like a tsunami.

It was messy. I had not been prepared for all this emotional stuff. I thought I was here to learn a hands-on therapy that would help relieve pain in my patients' bodies. Meanwhile, I sat about three-quarters of the way back in this huge lecture theatre, hiding in a sea of faces.

Having grown up in Northern Ireland during the 70s and 80s, I had safely hidden all my messy emotions deep inside, behind many layers of armour plating with bolts and padlocks and I had thrown away the keys. I didn't know how to let it out, even if I had wanted to.

In order to explain this further, I have to jump forward to share a powerful treatment I received at John's clinic in Sedona the following year. As you will see, I was hooked and ended up returning to America roughly twice a year for the next 5 years to continue my training.

I remember this specific treatment session at Therapy on the Rocks in Sedona. When the therapist became frustrated with my armour plating and asked me if it was me or my culture that just couldn't let go, I felt upset - like I was being told off. I immediately went back in time to my English class at school when I was about age 13. I could see my old English teacher shouting at me and telling me off for not being able to read out loud without stopping and stumbling over the words.

The therapist had not shouted at me or even raised their voice, but it somehow triggered this memory that I had held onto somewhere deep inside my body.

That evening when I went to bed, I woke in the middle of the night with a clear sense of panic. I felt totally out of my depth here in Sedona and thought I would never truly be able to let go of my walls of protection and trust what might lie beneath. All these thoughts, fears and emotions were bubbling just below the surface when I turned up the following day for treatment. My therapist chatted briefly about what I was feeling, as I tried to explain the jumble of emotions and panic going on inside my head and my body. They then asked me, 'what if we could go into that feeling of panic a little bit today, or a lot?' I felt safe in their hands and thought, what have I got to lose, these guys know what they are doing.

We dove in and I can't even begin to explain where we went...

There were tears, there was sobbing that sounded as if it wasn't even coming from me. That particular treatment and the next one were two of the most healing, armour-melting treatments I have ever experienced in my life. And there have been many.

The first therapist obviously pressed a button that needed to be pressed in order for me to begin to take down the thorny hedge I had spent years growing around myself. It was hard to let myself be seen with my messy lostness on full view. This journey took me to a place where I began to wrestle with my shadows. I was able to name them one by one.

I recognised their origins and, in doing so, it felt like I was pouring medicine onto my pain. Slowly, I began to invite others behind this hedge and to allow their healing hands to sink into the very depths of my soul. I accepted the challenge to let down my defenses and allow my vulnerability to surface. I felt heard. I felt held, supported and safe.

I was so used to bearing the weight of loss, rejection, fear and pain on my own, that I often fell back into that pattern. But I have learned that many hands do indeed make light work. The more treatments I received, the more open I became. It's not always easy for a heart that has been wounded to reach out for help.

It's only now, after years of working as an MFR therapist, that I understand when a patient reaches out, it is a generous offering to the therapist and a tremendous privilege to bear witness to their healing and courage in letting go. It has always been up to me, as the therapist, to create a safe and caring environment, to hold space for each patient and then to wait in love. It is always an honour to be part of their healing journey, no matter how messy it gets.

As a patient, it was only when I was willing to ask for help, that I witnessed a cascade of abundant healing being released in my body. But in order to do that, I had to let go of the fierce self-reliance that was preventing me from accepting what was being offered. My heart had spent too long shutting itself behind the armour, choosing not to trust, when really it was longing to be seen and to heal.

The path of healing is never linear. Indeed, everything in nature and in life has periods of contraction and periods of expansion. There will be times when we take great strides towards being in a better place, but there will also be times when we find ourselves under pressure. That's just life. Trust that these alternating periods are exactly what is needed to shape and mould us into who we are meant to be. It is this process that helps us to grow, to expand and to stretch to greater heights. It's important to acknowledge both the difficulties and the pain, while still honouring the onward call. For without this acknowledgment, we are unable to move forward. It's part of forgiving yourself for allowing those limitations to hold you back in the first place. We all do it. I like to look upon both giving and receiving treatment as a practice of generosity.

This amazing treatment helps to give a voice to something that has lost its voice.

It offers a loving touch to places that have never been caressed or held.

It gives belonging to that which never quite felt like it fitted in.

It provides shelter to the exposed.

Hearing and listening to the hidden stories.

Recognition of someone's pain.

Seeing to someone who has never felt seen.

Beauty where there has been trauma.

Forgiveness where there is hurt.

It gives value to someone's dreams.

Gentleness where there has been harm.

Hope where there has been hopelessness.

Comfort where there has been loss.

Feeling where there has been numbness.

Wisdom where there has been confusion.

For me, MFR has helped me to touch my own ungrieved parts and it has unearthed unknown depths.

EMBODIMENT

One thing I heard John saying was, 'come back into your body,' often followed by, 'you survived.'

I was coming to understand that sometimes life throws something at us that is so painful or traumatic that the only way we can cope at that time is to leave our body. Life can feel too hard, so we feel like we want to escape and, in extreme cases, you might even continue to live your life totally disconnected from your body. Walling our body off from our conscious experience forces us to ignore and neglect our body until it screams loudly enough to catch our attention.

It's not surprising that we sometimes want to protect ourselves from such a significant trauma. However, at some point, we have to come back in to fully inhabit our physical body in order to survive and thrive. This can be a very scary process, but one that allows us to fully heal. It requires us to truly feel what we have been avoiding for many years.

Too often we go through life living almost entirely in our heads, not just because of a trauma, but because our culture encourages it. We have a tendency to see the body as a housing for the mind, when we really need to embrace just how amazing, intelligent and wise our bodies are.

'How can we feel as if we belong to the wider

world when we don't even feel a true sense of

belonging to our own physical form?'

~Sharon Blackie[6]

If we fail to grasp this realisation about our own physical bodies, how can we ever hope to live in the wider world, missing out on so much joy and wonder? If we begin the journey of breaking free from the prison of our own heads, we can begin to listen to our bodies, hearing what our physical symptoms are trying to tell us. Such symptoms often tell us where we are holding tension, where the fascia has become solidified or stuck, where traumas or emotions are being held in the tissues. Then we have a choice. We can choose to ignore it and shove it down for a while longer, or we can choose to get treatment, to self-treat, to release it, and thereby actually help to resolve our symptoms.

I think most people when they stop long enough, realise that they have physical symptoms that are in response to stress, for example, headaches, stomach cramps, indigestion, or shoulder tension. Each person tends to hold tension in certain parts of their body. I hold mine in my neck, shoulders and jaw to name but a few. Our body has an important story to tell, if only we would listen. If we stop long enough to rest in the stillness, it can bring nourishment to the very cells of our body.

If we learn to fully inhabit our body, you'd be surprised at the wisdom that lies within.

Once we begin to treat our bodies with respect, we begin to see that they are actually brimming with life. And maybe we might just begin to like ourselves again. We might realise that our body is our companion on our journey through life. We can't do life without our body and, if we can lighten the load by listening, this communion will take us to a new level of knowing ourselves.

It hit me how I had been taking this body I had grown up in for granted. So if I wanted to create real, permanent change I needed to fundamentally shift the way I saw my body and my place in it. I needed to re-enchant myself, to fall in love with this complex and mysterious vessel. Then I might stand a chance.

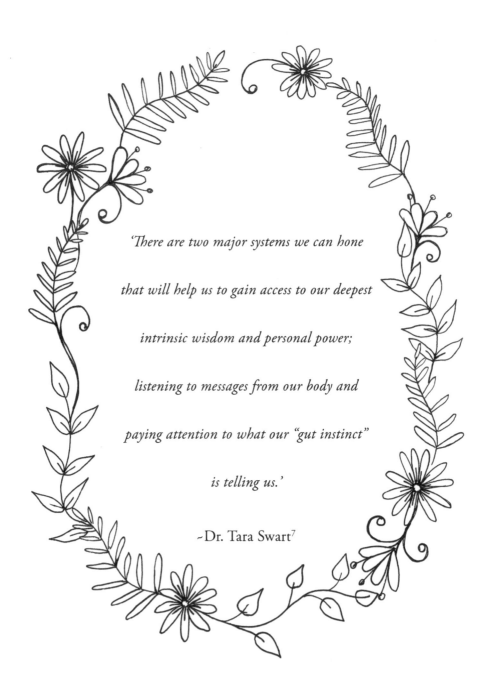

'There are two major systems we can hone

that will help us to gain access to our deepest

intrinsic wisdom and personal power;

listening to messages from our body and

paying attention to what our "gut instinct"

is telling us.'

~Dr. Tara Swart[7]

Where some may deem it woo woo, I see it as actually tuning in to the awareness that already exists throughout your body.

I began to see a shift in my understanding and beliefs that the body was just an object controlled by my mind, to realising that my mind or consciousness was located throughout my body in the fascial system. I was discovering that our bodies are way beyond any understanding I previously had, even after completing a Physiotherapy degree and working as a Physiotherapist for 25 years.

I felt something of a paradigm shift!

I had stumbled along for the first half of my life unaware of something called "inner wisdom", choosing to totally ignore my soul whispering as loud as it dared. As I experienced MFR, something began to soften. Something that had previously felt impenetrable in the area of my chest. As I found my way to my heart, I discovered a newfound respect for my body and all it had been through. I was learning how to more fully inhabit it. I started to feel more aware of how my body responds to different feelings and emotions, often resulting in my habitual pattern, which was to put up walls to protect. But I began to realise that I had a choice.

I could remain stuck in my pattern of shutting down, contracting and tightening or I could actually choose to let go, soften, open up and stand tall.

So I began to listen to my body and to respond when it spoke to me. To hear its stories. I'm learning that my body is in fact a storyteller, if only I would listen. Sometimes the voices are distant and sometimes they are an alarm call. I'm learning to listen for the soft whisper so that I don't have to hear it scream.

As I listened, I started to feel much more connected to my own body, with an accompanying sense of internal spaciousness and a simplicity which was no longer dominated by the agendas of society around me.

Self-awareness and self-treatment are like singing to your body, soothing it from the inside out. It's when you get to be generous and really listen to the state of your soul.

'*With awareness comes choice.*'

~John F. Barnes[8]

Self-treatment helps to bring resonance as we begin to release notes and melodies, singing our way home as we get to untangle, soften, open and release all that hinders our body from singing its own chorus of freedom, freedom that allows us to dance if we just take off our brakes and let go.

As we become more fully embodied, we will feel more fully alive. No longer just a spectator, but wanting to fling our arms wide open and embrace this one, beautiful life.

RETURNING HOME

My first intensive dive into the world of MFR, allowed me to complete three courses back to back in America, all made possible by my good friend Sandie allowing me to stay in her home in Cincinnati while attending the training. It was so lovely to come home each evening to home-cooked food and conversation, to try to put into words what I had learned that day.

Returning home to Northern Ireland however, was hard. I missed the new community I had become a part of. Slowly, these strangers had turned into friends, friends who have now stayed friends, continuing to support one another even miles apart. I found myself welcomed into the hearts and hands of so many different souls during those two weeks. I had experienced a kinship I will never forget. There had been an ease of friendship that was uncomplicated and clear. Indeed in the years that followed, I was overwhelmed by the kindness and generosity of strangers as they welcomed me into their homes, their own place of sanctuary and shared brief but intense moments of their lives with me.

Thanks to one such friend, Patricia, I was able to return to Sedona time and again, knowing I had a comfy bed and an open door into her home each and every time I attended for further training.

Having finished this initial training in Cincinnati, I left on a high of new knowledge gained, new understandings of how the body can heal itself, new friends for life and, in many senses, a new body of my own. When I returned home, I felt lighter, clearer, stronger and more alive than I had in

'I wish to live a life that causes my soul to

dance inside my body'

~Dele Olanubi[9]

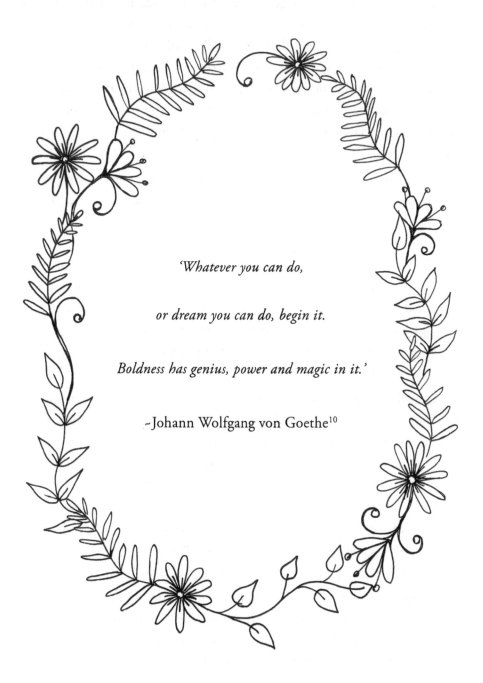

'Whatever you can do,

or dream you can do, begin it.

Boldness has genius, power and magic in it.'

~Johann Wolfgang von Goethe[10]

years. It felt as if I had managed to climb back inside my body and it felt good to be home, as if I actually belonged inside my body again. I began to hear a gentle voice, one that was louder and surer than all the other voices - the voice of my heart. I was learning to hear the voice of my own soul awakening inside of me. I also realised that I had virtually none of the symptoms I had struggled with for years. These symptoms were collectively labelled as post-viral fatigue or fibromyalgia depending on which doctor I had seen.

Of course, I felt joy and excitement with all this new understanding and healing. But I also felt very alone. I was worried about how my patients would receive it. Would they think I had lost the plot, as I stood still for five minutes or more applying such gentle pressure into their body? Would they be lying there thinking, what on earth is she doing? I worried about what patients would think. I worried about what colleagues would think. I worried if I really knew what I was doing. Would I get results? Would people unwind? Would they be willing to let down their guard? I have to be honest it was a bit of a rollercoaster ride but something deep inside me kept calling me to do the work and to trust in myself.

I slowly but surely began to introduce some MFR techniques into my treatments and, low and behold, when the patients returned, they would ask for more of it. It wasn't easy and often I would slip into a cycle of doubt. Doubting myself and my abilities as a therapist. Doubting if I really knew what I was doing. I began to let these doubts undermine me and would sometimes choose the easy option of doing what I knew, instead of stepping into the unknown. This cycle of self-sabotage almost became a defense against placing myself in a position where I might be rejected.

But still, when I did summon up the courage to try some MFR, the results were beyond my imagination or understanding. So I nudged into the challenge. Somehow as I pushed into the unknown, the self-doubt which was so deeply ingrained into me that it felt like scar tissue, began to soften. I continued to step towards that which frightened me and I began to catch glimpses of miracles along the way.

Practicing MFR can feel magical. With my eyes closed, I practise being fully present with my patient. I set my intention to help through my heart and bring my attention to where I feel restrictions, while I let my hands sink gently through the superficial layers of fascia. As soon as I feel resistance, I wait there. It can feel like I am almost caressing the fibres of fascia in such a way that they begin to sing, or resonate, or dance.

And where there might have been a tangle of life caught up in the fascial web, now there is a symphony or harmony which appears as my hands begin to melt further in. It feels like my hands become more fully enmeshed into those fibres as they sink through the depths. Each of our bodies contains the encapsulated wisdom of ages past. Our personal story is deeply enmeshed in those layers which I am learning to explore. The capacity and wisdom of our human bodies are totally beyond our understanding.

I remembered watching John as he placed his hands on each participant, taking time to make a connection. He did so by first finding a place of absolute presence, love, expansion, non-judgment, stillness and equality. There was no agenda and no expectation.

I was yet to learn the importance of detaching from the outcome, as I tried to listen to the fascia with my hands. At first, it felt like subtle changes beneath my hands, heat, tingling, pulsing. Then I started to clearly feel stuckness, tension, tightness, or resistance.

When treating my patients, I became less mechanical and more alive, as I weaved a curious act of intimacy by placing my hands on the body of another person. I had a newfound respect and understanding of what lay beneath their skin. As I continued with this work, I began to feel intrigue, instead of fear.

It can feel like a knowingness that I can't fully understand, but that I choose to trust. I was allowing what I had learned to unfold and bring liberation, expansion and truth, not only for myself but also for my patients.

I decided that I wanted to become more open, in order to fully experience all the voluptuousness that life had to offer. I sought to escape the rat race and instead focus life around the discovery of personal meaning and building further knowledge in this work. So, as I have said, I returned to America multiple times to take more courses and immerse myself in this new way of life. These trips to America became a sort of pilgrimage, a vision quest, a rite of passage that would show me the mystery and wonder of each person I met along the way. These people were like stepping stones - each one necessary. It was as if we were inextricably bound together, giving and receiving, speaking and listening, seeing and being seen, holding space for each other to heal and expand. We were all on this journey together, walking side by side.

Each time I returned home, however, I had to constantly make a conscious effort to disregard the sceptic in me and recall the amazing changes I had experienced, not only in my own body, but also in my soul.

I chose to commit to the process of growing, changing and becoming who I felt called to be, all fundamental to the art of living in this newfound state of healing and belonging. This discovery has shown me the importance of knowing that sometimes we have to step off the path we have been so determinedly striding along in order to learn something new. This alternative path was helping me to enter a place of rich teachings and to find a sense of rootedness.

This new path had been waiting to lead me back home. I knew it would be a winding path, but one that I would get to forge. It would be my very own path of becoming. This path was worthy of grasping. This way of thinking and being was so new to my world, but I took a deep dive and focused fully on this new way of working. Up until now, my treatment of patients had been very controlled and manipulated. The very opposite of these new practices of working in harmony with the body and never forcing.

Looking back to my university training, it now seems very linear and science-based. Treatments were very prescriptive, there was certainly no room for how a human soul might turn up on your treatment table. There was absolutely no mention of the possibility of the mind-body connection.

With doctors and physiotherapists treating the body and psychologists treating your mind. But I think this programming started even earlier when I was at school, being taught to label things and categorise them. Our education system forces us to adopt a position of separation and distance from others, as soon as we begin to learn. With us and them, right and wrong attitudes prevail. This system drives us to spend huge quantities of time locked inside our own heads, blinding us to the possibility that there is more to see and feel as life unfolds within and around us. Our education steals from us the understanding that we are all bound up in this together. We are a vast web of humans, animals and every aspect of nature - everything belongs. The Education System leaves no room for such things as intuition, wisdom, or gut instinct - these were all labelled as irrational.

I had to totally re-examine how I was working as a Physiotherapist - I was so used to getting in there and fixing the problem at a physical level. I had to really learn how to work with the body rather than against it. I had to learn how to detach from the outcome. I had to stop trying so hard. I had to stop treating people who didn't want to participate in the process, or who didn't want to form a relationship with their own body.

So many patients just come into the treatment room, lie up on the treatment table and want you to somehow fix them, without them having to do anything or change anything about their lifestyle that might just have brought them there in the first place. There are an increasing number of people around the world struggling to extricate themselves from the cycle of being prescribed another tablet, wanting that quick fix, feeling trapped with their own impatience. Desperate for change, but not knowing how to bring their lives back under control.

I had to accept that instant gratification and relief did not result in true healing, but instead, it requires patience to discover the wisdom that lies inside your soul. You cannot rush this process. Only when we give up the fight for control, do we let something beautiful take place. The soul gets a chance to reveal itself through subtraction - letting go! And in letting go, we allow an unfurling and opening inside of us which creates a deeper beauty on the inside. I have come to learn that it's only by forming a deeper relationship with your own body that you can really begin to address the crisis you might find yourself in right now. People have become so disconnected from their bodies that we no longer listen or feel into those dark spaces inside us. But when we do, it's as if a magical doorway opens up and your body becomes a safer place.

Once I started listening to my body, it was like coming back to what I had always known but had simply forgotten. It was as if I could come home. It's that sense of coming home to your own body, mind and spirit that is truly magical. It leaves you feeling a power and vitality that you didn't even know was possible. In order to heal and survive all that this life throws at us, we need to be part of the process. We can't expect it to just happen. All of us can find that relationship with our body if we take the time to really listen and feel. If we are patient.

I had found my new purpose. To teach people how to connect with their bodies and heal. It was like I had woken up to my body and I didn't want to fall asleep again.

FASCIA

After those initial 11 days of training with John F Barnes, in Cincinnati, my life was literally changing before my eyes. I began to catch glimpses of something new, a new way of thinking, feeling and loving, began to emerge. Perhaps the first thing I had grasped was just how amazing our bodies are. How they function in ways that I had never comprehended. My understanding up to that point had been so linear and limited. Attending this training had just blown the lid off the box in which I had been living. So let me backtrack a little here and try to explain:-

Fascia is an incredibly strong connective tissue that spreads throughout our body in a three-dimensional web, much like a spider's web. It extends from head to toe without interruption. Fascia supports, protects, envelopes and becomes part of every muscle, bone, nerve, organ and blood vessel

right down to the cellular level. That is, it surrounds every cell in our body. It is the life force of our body, bringing nutrients to each and every cell.

When the fascia is healthy, it is soft, fluid-filled and mobile. However, it can become hard, stuck and congested, causing huge compressive forces through pain-sensitive structures anywhere in our body. Trauma (which can be either physical or emotional), inflammation, or infection causes the fascia to reorganize along lines of tension, and by doing so it tightens down and solidifies. This excessive pressure from myofascial restrictions can produce pain and cause havoc in our bodies. MFR treatment helps to remove the straitjacket of pressure caused by restricted fascia, thereby eliminating symptoms such as stiffness, pain, headaches, spasm and fibromyalgia, as well as restoring freedom of movement.

John talked about how we, as therapists, have learned in a very linear, logical and intellectual way. But how in MFR, we need to tune in more to our essence, our creative, intuitive, feeling and inner wisdom, sides that we all have but have forgotten how to use. Throughout our education, these creative, intuitive and wise parts of ourselves have been stifled and shut down.

The MFR approach to healing includes aspects of our mind and our body and its powerfully creative healing potential. It was so completely different from the methodical forcing of the patient's body that I had been used to for more than 25 years. Suddenly, I was being taught to allow my hands to gently sink into the fascia and to honour each barrier, never forcing through. To honour and wait patiently until the tissues invite us in further. So often we forget that there is a whole landscape inside us.

How often do we stop and think about what lies beneath our skin? There is a vast interconnected luminous network that holds us up, supports us and brings life to every cell and molecule in our bodies. Each cell being inextricably enmeshed in this life-giving web. We are indistinguishable from our own distinctive internal landscape.

Each of life's experiences leaves a mark on that landscape, shaping who we are. We become an entanglement of our story.

MFR shines a light into that internal landscape, highlighting the unique mysteries inside each one of us. Each place is approached carefully and with respect. If you allow it, it will uncover areas of boundedness. We can choose to dive deep and come face-to-face with the mystery held inside or we can choose to turn away. We don't need to make sense of it or find meaning in it. Instead, choosing to fully inhabit our body and not to escape it, knowing that our internal landscape not only shapes us but dictates how well our body functions. We can choose to dive deeper and the resulting sense of homecoming will leave us feeling so much more whole. We become something more than we otherwise could ever have hoped to be. So we welcome those entanglements, knowing that as they soften, release and flow, we are becoming something both greater and infinitely more interesting.

Remember that sometimes, it is in the most challenging places that we are taught our greatest lessons. After all, this vessel that holds us and nourishes us deserves no less of us than to truly make it our home.

The fascia, much like a cobweb, catches passing flies or bugs for the creator of the web to feast on. The fascial web in our body also captures passing emotions and memories associated with traumas that impact our lives. These memories are stored in the tissues of our bodies. This is called Tissue Memory or the "fascial voice". Often, where these memories or emotions are held, there will be restrictions. And often when the restrictions are released, so too are the emotions associated with those memories. Patients can cry, get angry, make noises, or scream. The therapist encourages them to let this happen. They don't have to work it all out, in fact, the more they can stay away from thinking and trying to work it out, the better. Instead, if we can just trust what our body is doing and allow it to release what it is trying to get rid of, then healing will occur. Sometimes, the body will begin to move spontaneously or unwind into a position of past trauma in order to get a better release of the trauma it has held onto for too long. Every physical trauma carries an emotional component. I must admit at the start, it really challenged my beliefs. I felt a bit stuck inside my own head, but at the same time, I felt drawn to lean in and learn more. It felt inexplicable but deeply compelling. This was all news to me. I had no idea the body was capable of any of this.

My first experience of tissue memory was when someone was practicing a Psoas release deep in my abdomen. It was intense, despite her gently sinking in through the layers of restrictions in this area. As I tried to feel the discomfort and soften, rather than brace against it, I became aware of an intense pressure at the back of my jaw. I tried to soften and not clench my teeth together, but the pressure became so intensely painful, I felt like someone was pulling my back teeth out. How could this be happening? The therapist was nowhere near my head or mouth.

Afterward, my legs were shaking uncontrollably as I sat in the sea of participants and John answered any questions. I had to speak up, despite everything inside me crying out to me to remain quiet. Somehow I got my question out, 'John, how come when my partner was working on my tummy, I felt like someone was literally pulling my teeth out?' Immediately, he asked me if I had ever had any dental surgery. Yes, I had all four wisdom teeth out and a tumor removed from the roof of my mouth when I was 22. The surgery was extensive at the time and there was a skin flap to cover the hole left once the tumor had been removed. John simply said, 'Yes, so the tissues and your mouth are remembering the trauma of the surgery.'

Because the fascia is continuous throughout your body, sometimes, when you are releasing fascia in one area, it will highlight another area of deep restrictions elsewhere in the body. This blew my mind, but at the same time, it made so much sense.

As a therapist, my goal is to mould with and listen to each of my patient's bodies, so that I can help them release restrictions that are lodged inside of them. The patient will be led to the edge, to the barrier of their restrictions and then we wait there together. This is the place of opportunity but it's totally up to the patient to decide if they trust their own body enough to let go and dive deeper. Healing comes in many forms, but only with an awareness. Where there is no awareness or no feeling, there will be no healing.

After physical trauma or surgery, one of the biggest insults to our fascia is fear. Fear causes our fascia to solidify, keeping us entombed in old patterns of living life. Fear kills and confines all that is vibrant and alive inside you. Fear alone can cause multiple restrictions that wreak havoc in your body. Learning to let go of fear and where you hold it in your body will bring change and transformation not only to your body, but also to how you experience life.

MFR provides a whole-body treatment that is far more profound than just a 'different' treatment option.

'Our body is precious,

it is our vehicle for awakening.

Treat it with care.'

~Buddha[11]

CHAPTER FOUR

Weird and Wonderful

WHAT'S TRAPPED IN YOUR WEB?

Every single one of us has the ability to truly know our own body, but so often we choose to remain blind. The truth is, it's up to us and us alone to make better choices about how we treat this vessel that carries us through life. We each get to choose whether or not we ignore those butterflies in our stomach or those tense, tight shoulders or that clenched jaw in bed at night. It's up to us to decide to actually pay attention to our body. So please hear me when I say that your body can tell you its stories, if only you would listen. We all carry our stories inside our bodies. As we experience traumas, fears, grief, doubt, or loss, these stories are held in our fascia.

Even the stories others project onto us can be held inside, as are the stories we tell ourselves. Stories that might not even be true.

Through this journey of discovery, I have realised that I have spent my whole life trying to hide what was in my web. Choosing to shove down my emotions and ignore my body as it tried desperately to get my attention. I was trying to hide who I was, hiding my depression and swallowing my

'Every cell in your body

is eavesdropping on your thoughts.'

~Bruce Lipton[12]

grief. I was worried that if I let myself feel what was going on, that I would somehow explode and that I wouldn't be able to pick up the pieces. It always felt easier to not revisit any of the darkness for fear of getting stuck there. But MFR has helped me see that there is another way and it has given me the courage to dive in.

On a deeper level, I have come to realise that my relationship with my body cannot heal until I listen to each of its stories. For there are many layers of stories held right here inside my body. Stories of trauma, both physical and emotional, are held in the web of my fascia. Some deep, while others are closer to the surface.

Let's talk 'tissue memory', as I have briefly mentioned in the previous chapter. Yes, there is such a thing where memories of events, good and bad, are held in the tissues of our body and not just in the cells of our brain. The first time I heard this talked about, I must admit, I was pretty sceptical. Despite my reservations, there are multiple reports and documented cases of organ transplant recipients reporting inherited memories, experiences and emotions of their deceased donors. There was one particular case I heard about that made me realise this was actually a real thing.

I read about an eight-year-old girl who had received the heart of a murdered ten-year-old girl and she began to have recurring, vivid nightmares about the murder. Eventually, the details of these nightmares were shared with the police. Such specific descriptions and details were given and used as evidence in court, resulting in the arrest and conviction of the murderer. I realised tissue memory is a natural and normal occurrence.

On a simpler level, remember back to the last time you were very sick. Then think about what happened the next time you smelt or tasted the type of food you had eaten just before you were sick. I bet you had that sick feeling in your stomach again, felt queasy, or even felt the saliva start to pool in your mouth again. So, it's clearly normal for your body to have a physical response to a memory.

When fascia is released through touch, tissue memory can be triggered in the process, with emotions or sensations flooding to the surface that are connected to a particular memory from your past. This is exactly what happened to me when a therapist was releasing my Psoas area. I started to feel the actual trauma of the surgery in my mouth. Even though it was scary, I knew I was safe, and the more I could soften into the sensations I was feeling inside my body, the more my body would be able to let go and release the trauma that had become trapped in the fascia.

INTERNAL LANDSCAPE

We all carry our own unique tapestry of pain, darkness and light. It's waiting to be seen, it's waiting for someone to listen. We tend to shove the shadows down deeper, trying to ignore them, trying to push through. I had become an expert at it. But then it hit me that it felt like I was living life under a shroud of fog. However, I also understood that we have a choice: we *can* break the spell and lift the fog.

Our internal landscape is the result of our old stories. We can't ignore what has happened in our past but we don't have to let it colour our future. As we remember our past stories, we have the opportunity to walk through our landscape and help to weave a new story. This task requires us to be brave, to bring awareness into the vastness and darkness of that internal landscape, our fascia, and to see how its patterns came into being. MFR taught me how to do this and so much more.

Receiving an MFR treatment is not like any other hands-on treatment, where you just lie there and do nothing. The best way I can describe it is that you have the opportunity to travel deep within your own body. It's an inner journey where you get to really see, discover and feel your very own inner landscape. It's a journey where we get to bring a torch to shine a light into all our cracks and crevasses. Where we get to listen to our inner voice, our intuition, our essence and we get to become our most authentic self.

'Only when we are brave enough

to explore the darkness,

Will we discover the infinite power

of our light'

~Brene Brown[13]

If we are brave enough to let go and leap from the surface, into our greatest depths, if we have the courage to explore the depths of knowing within, then nuggets of gold might just be revealed.

As I became accustomed to receiving MFR treatments, I was able to feel areas of tightness and solidity in my body with increasing interoception[14]. These are the places I now bring my attention to, trying to soften and let go, hoping to bring more fluidity and freedom into these areas of bracing that existed in my body. The only way I can describe it is that these areas where we hold tension or repetitively brace in our bodies become dark, heavy and stuck, obstructing the flow of nutrients, life and light into each and every cell.

MFR gave me the tools not only to help me change my internal landscape but also to even realise I had one. I began to feel new life rising from the darkness and see beauty in these unfamiliar places, places that I had chosen to ignore, to bury deep inside. Amidst all the rubble, I knew I had lost the part of me that was crying out to be seen. So I chose to trust what I could feel pushing through the darkness, like a flower bud pushing up through the soil beneath.

A change was calling forth from my soul, bringing new creativity and alignment. Changes in my fascia began to transform my inner landscape into new fertile soil.

With my walls now starting to come down, I was becoming the newness I had been crying out for. It was by no means easy and required me to walk into places I feared. But as I entered, it felt like I was able to bring light into all those tight corners, calling forth the mysteries inside and finding more of me.

Choosing more love and light helped me grow in the direction of my heart, filling every part of me with liquid light. Creating this new landscape within me meant I was able to birth new dreams.

I felt new inspiration, creativity and clarity about the way I wanted to do life. This experience was only possible for me as I began to learn how to connect with my body. We all spend way too much time imprisoned in our heads, caught up in our thoughts, rushing from one thought to the next and totally ignoring our bodies in the process. Then we wonder why our bodies get into the state that we often find ourselves in, full of pain or dysfunction. If this experience had taught me one thing, it was that I didn't want to keep ignoring my body. I certainly did not want to end up in this state of numbness and pain ever again.

MFR has taught me how important it is to take time daily to come out of my head and into my body. To have no thoughts or thinking and just be in the pure sensation of my internal landscape in order to sink into its depths.

By doing this, we can immediately feel parts of our body that are bracing or holding, even as we are trying to let go and let our body melt like butter. I guarantee you will always find somewhere that you are still bracing even when you feel you are totally relaxed.

When I get into bed at night and think I am relaxed, I often find that I am not fully letting the weight of my head sink onto the pillow or that my jaw is still clenched tight. Once we are aware of these holding or bracing patterns, then, and only then, do we have the choice to let it go. And if we don't come out of our head and into our body then we will not feel or be aware of what is going on with our body in the first place.

It's in these areas that we need to travel in order to discover what it is we're holding onto and what it is that we need to let go of.

So if you are lucky enough to ever receive an MFR treatment, instead of lying on the treatment table thinking about what you're going to make for dinner, I challenge you to come out of your head and into your body, listening to the stories that your body is trying to tell you. It was only through such treatments that I began to see just how much tension I held in my body, how much bracing was going on when I felt any threat, vulnerability, or fear. As I learned to let go and soften my body, it felt like night and day.

I realised just how much I had been bracing through life and just how much more I needed to let go and release.

I think a lot of this pattern of bracing started when I was about 9 years old. When I survived the bomb blast in our home.

This experience has caused me to brace against life.

Always wanting to be good.

Wanting to please others.

Never speaking up.

Silencing my voice.

Avoiding conflict.

Then, after Dad left, my life became consumed with fear, sorrow, loneliness and anger, each forming yet another layer of armour around my heart.

When I received further intensive treatment, I knew it was time for this warrior to let her armour melt. If I was ever going to catch a glimpse of the real me, I had to let go of these layers of armour and bracing I had built up over the years. It was messy when I had to walk right into the emotion and pain. Sometimes, it felt like I was going to break open. The armour I had built around me made me somehow feel safe. It was scary to even think of cracking it open. I was scared to see what really lay beneath. However, I knew deep inside, that this armour was not only blocking the light, but it was creating darkness. My soul was crying out for the light; she had had enough of the darkness. My essence was slowly dying without the light and the struggle had become exhausting.

As my armour began to break down, I actually realised that the light didn't come from the outside in, but that it strangely already lived inside of me. This light started to crack the armour from the inside out. It felt unbelievably liberating. As I grew in courage, the desire to shed this armour became unstoppable. Once I started to feel into my body, I was aware of feeling parts of me that I didn't even know existed. I began to understand that through the various traumas, I had actually disassociated from my body, or at least parts of it. I can quite honestly say that my body never really felt like home to me and only now was I beginning to see there was an option to really fully inhabit it. As I climbed back inside and took up residence, all the darkness began to flow out of my head, my jaw, my neck and my entire body.

A lot of this darkness was stemming from where I had a tumour removed when I was 22 years old. Worry had taken up residence in these tissues as I feared the tumour would grow back.

But now I released all of these constrictions, emotions and false beliefs, allowing the light to shine deeper into those cracks and crevices which were newly discovered. It felt like I was creating a place of beauty to call home, a place to actually belong. A deep knowing began to surface, one that told me I was made to be full of life, to be full of passion. I had the choice now to let that happen. I heard a whisper in my heart to let it go and to be alive. It was like all the sorrow and loneliness came out. It was noisy and messy. Memories flashing through my mind from childhood, from the teenage years and from adulthood. It felt like I was collecting parts of myself that I'd abandoned along the way in an attempt to survive all that life had thrown at me.

I was able to take back control, stand tall and look up. To feel at home and safe. To know I am loved, I am secure and that, despite everything, I have survived.

We always have more layers of armour to shed - it's never fully done.

We are human, after all. So, I no longer feel like I'm failing when I get lost in the shadows again. I am gentle when fear chokes me. I take special care to show myself love, even when I get stuck in those dark corridors of my being.

I am growing to love all the places I've never dared to go. Having the courage to restore love where I need it the most. I am learning to place my hand on my heart and whisper,

'I love you'

'I see you'

'I'm listening.'

Now, I see my body as a container that can hold and nurture me as I begin the process of reconnecting to my soul. It offers me an open-armed embrace, where I can dissolve, go to seed and regerminate. A place to be still and grow new roots. A place where I can cry or scream if I want. A place where I can begin to heal all that is wounded and recover all that is lost. A place where I can find my true self. A place to come home to myself.

No matter how much I think I've grown or changed, my default setting is always to make myself small. I hate being the centre of attention. I tend to hold myself at a distance, even from the people I love. But slowly, bit by bit, I have started coming home to my Centre.

Opening all that is closed within me.

Freeing myself from all that hinders.

Journeying to the centre of myself and sitting with the peace that is deep inside.

TRAUMA

We are fundamentally changed by trauma, not only psychologically but also at a cellular level. The body becomes inextricably entangled and tethered by our fears. It is no longer able to expand, flow and move freely as it is so beautifully designed to do.

Our story can cause biological changes to occur as our body keeps the score.

Every single human has a true genuine authentic self somewhere inside, but trauma disconnects us from it. Trauma, meaning what happens to us on the inside as a result of what happens to us in life. We can become disconnected because it's too painful to be ourselves. Healing is where we get to reconnect with our soul and realise we are the one we've been looking for all along, hidden behind our trauma. Healing allows us to come home, to belong to our authentic soul.

If growing up in Northern Ireland, in a border village during the height of The Troubles, had taught me anything, it had taught me how to brace with the sound of each bomb blast. It had taught me how to dive for cover. These experiences caused me to build my armour, layer upon layer, in order to survive. This armour involved fitting in, not standing out. It included toeing the line, being a good girl and going to church. Each layer buried the real me. It also meant that from a young age, I was living life on high alert 24/7, even if I wasn't aware of it. All this fear is held in our bodies as darkness and solidity. Compressing and crushing our organs and pain-sensitive structures. Fear is solidified fascia. My culture had allowed its thorny brambles and vines to hold me down, to tell me I had to bury stuff deep inside, to just forget it and push on through, to suppress my emotions, my fears and to ignore the fact that I felt threatened and unsafe growing up. We all just grew to accept that these daily atrocities were part of life. Life was consumed and surrounded by The Troubles. Little did I know that each of these traumas and emotions had become entombed in the fascia of my body.

I am so thankful that MFR has shown me the importance of travelling deep inside your own body where the fascia has moulded itself around our very own stories, forming the internal landscape we have today. MFR has revealed those deeply ingrained stories in me that it's time to let go of, in order to heal, grow and thrive. As I do so, I come to realise that I already have everything I need inside of me. It is crystalised deep in the marrow of my bones and inside every cell. Sometimes, we have to search through the rubble to find what it is we need to let go of and what we want to hold on to - letting go of the darkness and holding on to the colour and the light. I am learning to trust myself, to let go and allow this magical healing process to unravel, causing me to change and grow.

I began to ask myself:

Why do I sometimes feel nervous and doubt myself?

Why do I silence my true self?

Why do I fall into driven and perfectionistic patterns?

Why do I avoid conflict?

Why am I afraid to rock the boat?

Why do I push myself so hard to fulfill outward expectations?

Why does it matter so much that I please everyone?

It felt like all of these thoughts were emanating from my wounds.

All a part of the stories I had been telling myself for so long that I believed each one was true. I knew that by pursuing this journey, there would be so much to unravel and so much to unlearn. I also knew that it would be so worth it, as I listened to my body calling me home.

UNWINDING

During one of my early MFR treatments, I realised that the noise I could hear in the room was actually me. I was crying. It was a loud, hard, guttural sob and it was filling the room. It sounded like a little girl allowing all the loss, the loneliness and the rejection out, after holding it deep inside her bones. By letting go and allowing this noise to be released, it felt like I had somehow found the strength of my own vulnerability. And she began to raise her head and climb out of the cavernous place I had hidden her for over 40 years. I no longer wanted these feelings to be the blood songs in my body. I wanted to let them go. I realised I had hidden this little one, who deserved kindness, comfort and love, deep down in the sadness. I had chosen to abandon her. She was a part of me and as I melted the hardness in my body, I began to make room for her. Space for her to raise her head, stand tall and become a vital part of me today. I was creating a place for her to belong and to be loved.

When we learn to trust our body and fully let go, we are surrendering to its wisdom. Sometimes this means that our body might start to move into a position of past trauma or it might twitch or shake. These are all forms of unwinding and it's basically the body's wisdom allowing the body to do exactly what it needs to do to unravel restrictions, or release trapped energy or emotions. We don't need to work it all out, but just trust that our body is getting rid of something that no longer serves us. These are the moments that bring great healing if we trust what sometimes feels out of our control. The therapist will always keep you safe and you are always in control and can stop your body from doing what it is doing at any stage.

This unwinding is where language fails to describe what you are feeling or what emotions might flood to the surface. Unwinding allowed the little girl inside of me to find a language, to scream, releasing the rage, the sadness, the pain and confusion. No longer allowing these trapped emotions to eat at me from the inside.

Closing my eyes, my body heavy, my limbs going limp, letting go. I started feeling so light I could float, journeying deep inside layer upon layer, letting go. Then the movement begins. A twitch here and a floating limb there, my body takes on its own story of unwinding and letting go of tightness, bracing and emotions, all stuffed so deep inside I had no idea they were in there. I now know they had been there for years and years.

I travelled to a place where there is a little girl, not old enough to know her own fear, her anger, her terror. The sound of shattering glass, eardrums exploding, body crumpling, diving for cover, shaking… in the aftermath of a bomb.

Afterwards, somehow I feel more complete, more embodied. I can feel more of my essence inhabiting my body, shining through as the clouds begin to shift. My soul feels more complete, more whole like I've somehow retrieved a little piece of what was missing. It feels like an awakened understanding of who I am. Only now am I able to honor who I was created to be.

After such a life-changing experience, I was desperate not to return to using distractions to avoid or check out, as I had done for years. Instead, a longing lingered in the air, to more fully discover the truth of who I am. Unwinding feels like you are experiencing the mind, body, spirit connection all at once in a very mystical way. It is transformative. For me, it was a huge shift in consciousness, where I could sense the flow of life in the very cells of my body and beyond. As I learned to trust my body with gentleness and openness, I let it move in the patterns of the air around me. I felt weightless as I let go and allowed my body to unclench. Unwinding is like a dance between my body and my soul. It is my soul's own unique interpretation of what my body needed in order to process and let go of traumas that had been stuck deep inside for too long.

Each physical and emotional trauma felt like it had become a part of me influencing the shape and flow of my life, long after the event. But now I was discovering a way to release and let go of the baggage that I no longer wanted to carry.

After some MFR treatments which took me deep inside myself, I felt my inner landscape rearranging to such a degree that my perspective on life changed and it simply wasn't possible to turn back or resume the life I had been living. I chose to trust and allow both my body and my future to unfold in their own way. By letting go of control, of protection, of fear, I was able to further my own richer self-realisation. It's like turning within to find the very pulse of your soul, where you discover an awareness you didn't know existed. I was learning to stand in the midst of this aliveness. It deserved my attention, my respect and my care. It deserved my awe and my reverence.

For so long, I had not participated in any aspect of my body other than hating it and being so uncomfortable in my own skin. But now I could see and feel there were patterns, webs and weavings of something new moving all through me. I was enchanted with this beautiful mystery that was me, fluid and transforming in a constant process of becoming.

'In the process of letting go

you will lose many things from the past,

but you will find yourself.'

Deepak Chopra[15]

As I tried to explain all of this to my husband Peter, it was hard to find the words. In those early days, it was hard to understand it fully myself.

Then I noticed that there was a Healing Seminar being run that October in Sedona. This was a short 3-day seminar that John ran specifically for therapists and their family members to attend together. What better way or place to celebrate our 25th Wedding Anniversary than for both of us to attend. Peter jumped in with both feet. He had previously done some sensory-motor training as a counsellor, so he totally got the whole mind-body connection and the body keeping score of trauma theory.

Even when John played loud music and encouraged us to Jiggle (a standing exercise that helps loosen you up and increases the fluidity of our fascia), Peter was totally into it.

The days were just half days, so we also got to experience some of the breathtaking scenery when we set off on some stunning hikes. One such hike was up to the top of Cathedral Rock. It was more of a climb but it was so worth it for the views at the top. Two years prior there is absolutely no way I would have ever made it to the top! Once we had reached the peak and caught our breath, we wandered around to take in the view from every angle. As we came around a corner, we spotted someone in pain. This poor guy had found a quiet spot to quickly relieve himself before he headed back down the rock face but unfortunately, as he had squatted, he had somehow positioned his backside just a little too close to a cactus, managing to get some of the cactus needles stuck in his bum. He was groaning in pain and looking desperately for his wife. Peter and I did a quick turn and headed back out to the main viewing point. As we walked in this direction I spied a lady obviously looking for someone she had lost. She said she was looking for her husband. I said I think he's round the corner there but I think he's had a bit of an accident and might need some help. The poor man, those cactuses are brutal. Peter and I smiled at each other but at the same time, we could feel his pain.

The following day as we returned for the last day of the healing seminar. I vividly remember that afternoon as John led us through another unwinding experience. There was a lady in the room who was definitely going for it. The noise became louder and louder. I could hear John saying someone sounds like they're having way too much fun here. Peter looked at me and asked, "Is she having an orgasm?"

This was Peter's first-ever experience and introduction to the world of Myofascial Release. But miraculously, he continues to let me treat him!

Free To Soar

My sacred life is a journey
To find the soul beneath
Beneath all the roles life has put on me

Unearthing beauty
Allowing myself to come alive
Always changing

Trusting in the unseen wisdom
Pressing through my own skin

Imagining my knowing into being
Having the courage to do what is being born from me
Rather than what is imposed, expected

Breaking free from the "should" cage
Removing the weight from my wings so I can fly

A new order of things being born inside
Creating a new blueprint
With room to grow
While still belonging

Stepping, evolving into my journey of becoming
Becoming held and free
Free to soar

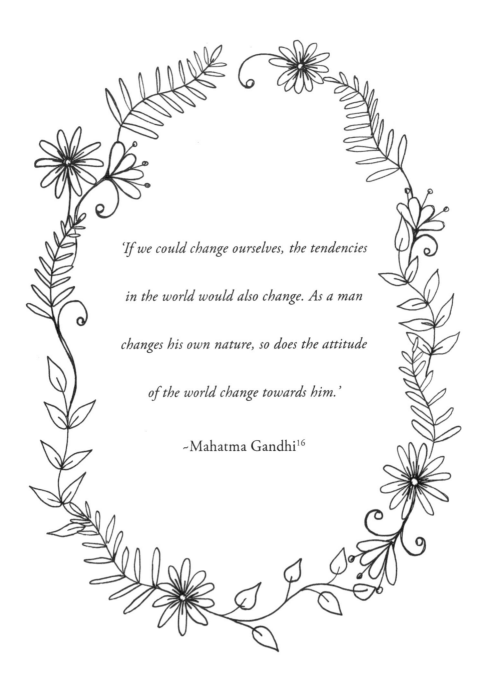

'If we could change ourselves, the tendencies

in the world would also change. As a man

changes his own nature, so does the attitude

of the world change towards him.'

~Mahatma Gandhi[16]

CHANGE

MFR has given me the courage to make my own choices and decisions. It is showing me that I do not have to stay on the path I had grown up on. The path that said I had to be good, successful and work hard.

Instead, I felt more than anything that if I stayed on that path, I would be burnt out and in chronic pain for the rest of my life. I knew I no longer wanted to run a business, manage staff and treat so many patients on a daily basis. This path was sucking the life out of me.

I can't remember where I read the following words but they jumped off the page so I recorded them in my journal. I later discovered they are a quote by Aldous Huxley[17]:

It's dark because you are trying too hard.

Lightly child, lightly.

Learn to do everything lightly.

Yes, feel lightly even though you're feeling deeply.

Just lightly let things happen and lightly cope with them.

I was so preposterously serious in those days...

Lightly lightly - it's the best advice ever given to me...

So throw away your baggage and go forward.

There are quicksands all about you, sucking at your feet,

trying to suck you down into fear and self-pity and despair.

That's why you must walk so lightly,

Lightly my darling...

I needed to take steps to change what I could.

My soul began to whisper, 'You've got this, you know exactly what to do.' I knew deep down that this moment of clarity would require action, otherwise it would float away like an autumn leaf in the wind. My choices and actions that followed would indeed be a pivotal moment in my life.

My dream was to create a smaller, quieter healing space. More in keeping with MFR. A place where my patients would feel safe to really let go if they wanted to. I wanted to see fewer patients in a day so that I didn't feel exhausted by the end of each day. I knew it was time for a change when I began to feel trapped. I was filled with inner conflict but knew deep down that running a busy clinic was quite simply not my place any longer. I needed the freedom to write a new story. I didn't have to continue doing what society expected of me. I now had the freedom to actively challenge the stories I thought I had to journey through and the paths I thought I was expected to travel. I wanted more than anything to recover the authentic wisdom which had been buried in the darkness. I was learning to somehow hold on to my truth now that I had found it. I slowly gained the courage to overcome the fear of being seen to fail, knowing that by staying and toeing the line I would be failing myself. Many people thought I was mad selling a busy thriving practice, but my inner voice kept saying, 'let go of security in order to grow'.

It was by no means an easy, straightforward transaction but I sold my practice around 4 years ago and have never looked back. It felt like such a weight off my shoulders. I then set up a beautiful, peaceful space at home, The Garden Room, where both my patients and myself love to come to remove some of the weight from our wings so we can fly.

CHAPTER FIVE

Soulfooting

PARALLEL PATHS

As I began my journey into the world of Myofascial Release (MFR), I also began to question my perception of who or what God was to me. It felt like these two journeys began at exactly the same time. Like I was travelling along two parallel paths at the same time. One path gently dismantled everything I had grown up believing with regards to God and Christianity, while the other path questioned so much of what I have been told about how the human body functioned.

Both paths would reveal so much more than I could ever have imagined, both taking me on a journey that I will never regret.

I had grown up deeply entrenched in the systems of religion and church, believing I had no other choice but to accept all that was taught to me. It was when I attended class after class of MFR training, where I began to witness beautiful souls all around me touching others with gentleness, love, healing, and compassion, despite a wide variety of beliefs and backgrounds, that I started to struggle with my rigid beliefs. It felt like

'Unknowing is part of faith.

Unlearning is part of growing up.'

~Kent Dobson[18]

my beliefs were pulling me knee-deep into sinking sand. While all around me there was a depth of warmth calling me forward into a new dimension of understanding.

As I journeyed these two parallel paths of MFR and faith, all I felt was overwhelming love crashing over me again and again. It was not an easy or straightforward journey, and yes, at times, I felt like I was being pulled under. The struggle was real! Sometimes I felt like I was losing my faith or even losing my mind, as all I thought I knew for sure came crumbling down around my feet. But somehow I kept surfacing, to a place where I was blinded by love and light. My soul felt more alive with love on the inside, as I broke free from the boxes into which I had put both God and myself.

There has been no lightning bolt moment on this journey, but slowly something somewhere was trying to get my attention. I sensed the pressing of something unseen, like a relentless hunch deep inside my soul, that I could no longer ignore.

I knew my reality was about to change into something new. Something much more beautiful than it currently was. And yet, despite these feelings of being drawn to something exciting and new, I would still be consumed by worry and fear. There were times when I felt desolate. It felt like there was a bottomless pit inside me that would never be filled with answers, as I was asking myself the same questions over and over again.

Was I losing my mind?

How could I no longer believe what I had grown up believing with every fibre of my being?

Was I going to hell?

Was I a heretic?

What would my family think?

Would they understand my scattered thoughts?

I was struggling to understand what was happening inside my own head, never mind being able to verbalise it to someone else!

'There is no birth of consciousness

without pain.'

~Carl Jung[19]

Would my friends abandon me?

Or was their friendship more than faith-based?

Despite all my worries and fears, I still felt compelled to discover who I was meant to be before the world took hold of me and told me who to be.

It felt like a slow but serious detox from all the expectations that had been placed on me throughout my life so far, as I began to evolve into me. I no longer wanted to remain 'fitting in' by staying small and broken. I was beginning to imagine a truer, more beautiful way to believe. I was becoming open to something new. I understood this would require constantly surrendering, letting go, as I emerged into this something new.

A door had opened that would bring transformation to my mind, my body, my emotions and my soul all at the same time.

FEAR OF CHANGE

As I have already said, this journey was not plain sailing. I noticed that as I began to change and grow, it felt like a betrayal of the person I once was and the beliefs I had once held dear. But it also felt like I was beginning to see glimpses of something worth the risk of changing for.

I slowly began to realise that resisting the change and refusing to step into this journey would be me refusing life. Turning my back on my soul's calling. But somewhere deep inside, the thought of walking an alternative path to the one expected filled me with fear. My old fear was resurfacing, that once again I would be rejected. I was fearful of not belonging again, of being somehow shunned. Little did I know that this new path would bring me to a place I could call home, right here in my own body. I was about to discover who I was outside of the expectations of the world.

I decided to believe that I was lovable even when at odds with others.

I knew I needed to trust in my own voice, especially when it wasn't necessarily in agreement with everyone around me.

I wanted to learn how to stand by the younger me and to release her from the unnecessary guilt and shame that was choking my words.

I accepted that change would be frightening but resolved to change anyway. I knew I would lose friends but I also knew I had to be true to myself. After all, humans are made to grow and to change.

Biologically, we are changing every day of our lives. The world changes with every season. So why is it so hard for us as humans to accept and embrace change, to open our minds?

Growing up, there was a clear scale of conformity to measure up to - how to act, how to behave, what to believe - and I always chose to be the good girl and fit in. But now I was open to the fact that truths change.

I am still very much on a faith journey. I don't have all the answers. I haven't got it all worked out. But I'm realising it's not about having it all worked out, it's about trusting in the mystery of my ordinary life. It's about stepping towards something that always feels just out of reach, rather than settling for safe and always agreeing, in order to avoid conflict. This had become such an ingrained pattern for me growing up. But now I was choosing to shed some unnecessary beliefs in order to allow myself to participate fully in the great divine dance that is my life. My decision to leave the church was possibly one of the most difficult decisions I have ever made in my life. Yet, I felt compelled to honour an onward call, whilst still acknowledging all that my relationships within the church had given me. It was hard. It took time to grieve the loss of friendships. The loss of community was the hardest thing to come to terms with.

But I knew somewhere deep inside that this separation was necessary, as this community could no longer meet me where I stood.

Little did I know at the time that this tough decision would become a step towards a place of my true belonging. To be truly human does not mean that you must make yourself small. Rather, it is to recognise that we are all the same size and that it's our combined offerings that lift us up and strengthen us all.

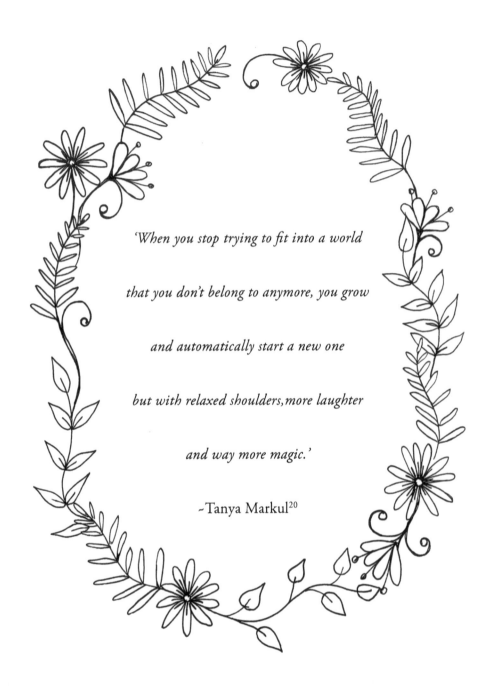

'When you stop trying to fit into a world

that you don't belong to anymore, you grow

and automatically start a new one

but with relaxed shoulders, more laughter

and way more magic.'

~Tanya Markul[20]

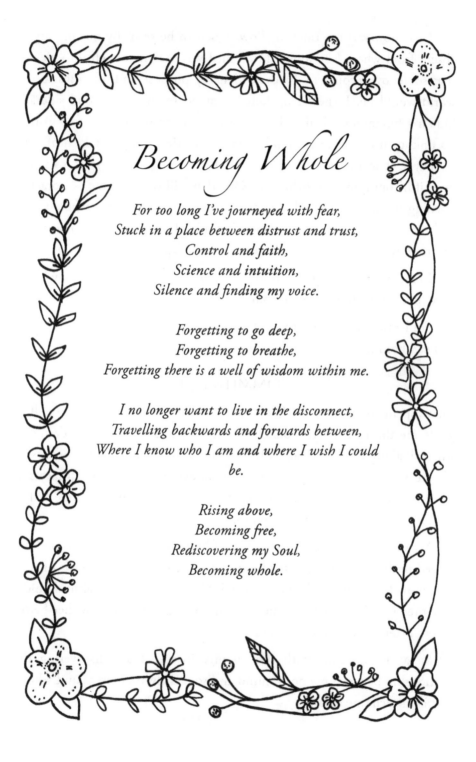

Becoming Whole

For too long I've journeyed with fear,
Stuck in a place between distrust and trust,
Control and faith,
Science and intuition,
Silence and finding my voice.

Forgetting to go deep,
Forgetting to breathe,
Forgetting there is a well of wisdom within me.

I no longer want to live in the disconnect,
Travelling backwards and forwards between,
Where I know who I am and where I wish I could
be.

Rising above,
Becoming free,
Rediscovering my Soul,
Becoming whole.

I felt now was the time to allow myself to be seen. By making myself absent from where I no longer fitted in, I was braving myself into view so that somehow I could re-discover what my purpose and offerings to this world would be. I knew I no longer wanted to show my good side and hide my humanity. I had a choice, to fake fitting in or to be free to turn up unknown depths and attend to my soul. Maybe it will take a lifetime or maybe it will sneak up on me, but I'm hoping and trusting to find a beautiful community to belong to. One that will welcome me as I practice opening my heart and find the courage to express my truth, where values and bonds weave us together, where strands of our stories become woven together, where there is space for each other's expansion and contractions.

In fact, so much of this already exists in the MFR community, where I have found myself welcomed from afar.

I'm learning, you have to be able to take hold of your own hand before you can hold the hands of others in community.

COMMITMENT

I have spent so much of my life looking to something outside of myself to guide me through. I have looked to religion; to success; to achievement, when all along what I was actually looking for was already inside of myself. We are all spiritual beings having a human experience. We are all facets of God; the Divine; the Universe or all that is. So we are always connected to it and it is always flowing through us.

My essence is my very own source of luminosity. It has spent too long buried under the many layers of armour, hidden behind the walls of fear. Somehow I'd forgotten she even existed. She is my wise and faithful guide, ever-present. Now, it's up to me to commit to getting to know her better and to listen to what she has to say.

So as I commune with the divinity in me, I am discovering the relationship between my body, mind and soul is always present and whole, as it is in each one of us.

'The breezes at dawn have secrets to tell you

Don't go back to sleep!'

~Rumi[21]

MEDITATION

We all long for meaning and purpose in this life we live. We search for ways to feel more at home. We know that this life will challenge us to become all that we could ever hope to be, if only we pause long enough to listen.

Before I discovered Myofascial Release and the magic of the mind-body connection, I was living life from the confines of my own head, consumed by my thoughts and thinking. I had forgotten how to feel or how to actually listen to my body. I was beginning to see how, in order to live a healthy balanced life, it required my whole-hearted participation of body, mind and soul in this adventure called life. I knew at times it wouldn't be easy, but I chose to believe that everything belongs. That every trip, stumble and fall, will in the end, create a richer tapestry of a life that is full of wonder and belonging.

I started to see how I had become so unaccustomed to making time just to be still, how I had stopped from engaging in the deeper dimensions of my body. Instead, caught up and consumed in my own thoughts, being trapped in this place in life was preventing me from not only listening to my body, but also from fully engaging with the world around me.

I've come to understand that we all have an invitational heart, it never stops inviting us to come home. If only we stop to hear its song singing us home. Sometimes just stopping isn't enough to allow us to hear what our heart, our soul, is trying to say. Often we have to sit in silence to really hear and to pay attention. Stillness can show us just how hospitable our body can be if we choose to sink into our very own internal landscape, taking time to notice what is held within, in those intricate fibres that weave our story into our body.

It's here, in the stillness of mind and body, where magic can happen. It opens us up to new possibilities, releasing fresh creativity, bringing freedom, offering a new sense of belonging and giving us a bigger perspective on this thing called life.

Meditation has been a great tool for me, to help me quiet my mind. I find it leaves me feeling lifted in spirit, nourished, new and fresh. It has become an essential part of my daily routine, if even just for 10 minutes. It helps me to come out of my head and into my body, bringing awareness to areas of tightness or tension. With that awareness comes choice - a choice to soften and let go. I once heard meditation described as a place where divinity and nature collide. There is so much power in that collision. It's a bringing together of all that there is. Meditation teaches me to bring more love and compassion into every day. It helps me to show up with a good heart and not just be in my head. It helps me to see the good heart in others and to see their beauty shining through.

There are many different forms of meditation and if you are trying to connect more with your body, I strongly recommend a body scan or guided relaxation meditation.

There are also many great apps, with a wide variety of guided meditations to suit everyone's taste.

MY TRUEST LIFE

I have no regrets about my church upbringing. In fact, it gave me a stable foundation to cling to when everything else in my life was falling apart in my early teens. I can see that everything has had its part to play in my journey. The fabric of our lives is woven from all the moments and events in our past, good and bad. I choose to reframe the painful past experiences in my life as necessary to have shaped me, choosing to write a good story out of the pieces I have been given.

My MFR journey has brought a new kind of freedom of body, mind, and soul. It's only now as I look back through a different lens that I can see that I was being forced into a cultural corset and a religious straight jacket, that was causing me to be stuck in a very black or white, right or wrong mindset. Only now am I ready, willing and able to become more of a yes/ and thinker, more of the person I was designed to be. Better late than never!

Once I opened the floodgates to a new way of thinking, it suddenly felt like I was being swept off my feet by a huge wave. But at the same time, I felt safe and supported, able to enjoy the freedom as I bobbed around in the ocean beneath me. It felt like a homecoming, after feeling so lost.

The absolute saving grace in all of this, that I haven't yet mentioned, was that my husband Peter was going through the exact same journey, with regards to faith, at exactly the same time as myself. In fact, he even had a head start. This was a true blessing, as I don't know if I would have had the courage to open myself fully, had he not been right by my side.

This whole experience broke me open to a point where it felt like an invitation to open myself even more to this new sense of wonder. It allowed me to reach beyond the restrictions I had been tethered by.

This wonder showed me how to encounter the world and beyond in all its beauty and mystery. I was beginning to see new possibilities of the Divine in me. It took confidence to speak my truth, knowing that anything or anyone I would lose by telling my story was never mine anyway. I decided I was willing to lose anything that required me to hide any part of myself. Slowly, I was able to imagine a truer, more beautiful path, belief and existence for myself, better than the life I had been living.

So instead of living life preparing for dying, a life full of judgment and striving to get it right, I realised I wanted to live this life open to changing, letting go and loving the newness found in each and every day. Open to learning and unlearning. I was prepared for the pain of unbecoming.

Free from apology, explanation, or justification, instead diving into growing and evolving.

Each one of us has the choice to live our truest life. Each one of us has a different version of what that truest life looks like and feels like. Who are we to judge others for the way they choose to live their life? Who are we to impose our beliefs on someone else? Our energy would be better spent concentrating our efforts on being true to ourself.

There's nothing more important than unearthing what we really believe to be true about ourselves and our world. Understanding that by doing the digging, there's a good chance that we will unearth deep-rooted beliefs that were not ours in the first place. So often our beliefs are programmed into us by culture, religion or authority figures, wherever we find ourselves growing up.

I was realising that remaining open to new possibilities would enable me to experience the world around me and within me, with a fresh pair of eyes. I was beginning to see things in new vibrant colours, so there was no going back to black and white. I was choosing to live life authentically, daring to be me. Living my truest life.

CHAPTER SIX

Belonging

REWRITE YOUR STORY

I've always found large family gatherings especially hard since Dad left. They make me feel overwhelmed - like I want to run and hide, so I don't have to look at the beauty surrounding me. It's like bearing witness to this beauty somehow feels too painful and I have seen plenty of that beauty in my husband's family, where getting together and family was always a priority for my amazing father-in-law, Brian.

Up until recently, I have needed my stories and patterns of bracing in order to feel safe. But I started to see that this brand of safety was leading to misery and that my body was trying to show me it didn't have to continue in this way. My MFR journey has revealed to me a deeper, truer meaning of the word safe, as I have come to realise that my walls of protection had turned into my jail. How come I felt so alone even in a crowded room? Perhaps it was time to let my defenses down and in doing so I knew that my past stories didn't have to define me or dictate my future.

Often, we become shackled to our past, remaining stuck in our story, choosing to live in this wasteland. But it's so important to remember that it's not what happens to you, but rather who you become in the face of what happens to you that counts. I'm learning that I always have options, a choice in how to react. Only then can I unshackle myself from my past stories, giving me the power to create a new story for myself. Excited to grasp that I am in an unending state of becoming.

I've grown to learn that the things that have shaped me, like grief, loss and rejection, can be where beauty resides, if we let it metabolise. As opposed to keeping it stuck and thereby creating a darkness in our soul that we continually try to ignore. It hit me that we can turn our pain into art, creativity, writing, or simply use it to encourage or offer compassion to others. However, the years of armouring and holding rigidity in my body, as I attempted to protect myself against pain or loss, can take a lifetime to melt away layer-by-layer. There is always a story under a story. Deep inside lies a memory of a memory. But if we begin to learn how to crack open our armour and allow the light to shine in, then our stories can be seen, heard and felt. Then we can begin to heal, as we get to choose to no longer let some stories we've been believing continue to live in our bodies as truth.

Rewriting your story isn't easy, because each day you have to wake up and choose to let go of the lie until it gets the message and stops trying to climb back inside your head. We have to remember that the stories we tell ourselves are merely interior thoughts that are often messed up; we repeat them over and over to no one but ourselves. And if we let them, they can become our reality. I knew it was time to stop telling myself the story of rejection. Being stuck in this story was causing me to continue the cycle of self-rejection. But now it was time to find a new way to walk, to find a new story to write.

I believe that true wisdom comes from reflecting on life, finding redemption in our own story. As I glance through the pages of my journals over the last 4 years, I begin to dream that maybe there is something held in those pages worth passing on. I take a step towards a new beginning as I start to string my words together, hoping to create something beautiful in the weaving.

Eventually, we all get to change our mantras and our behaviours, letting the old stories fall away as we realise we are not a bad person, we are enough, we are loved.

Writing has helped me accept that I am enough!

As we unbury the sound of things we have buried inside our body, things buried so deep that our mind tells us they have been forgotten, we get to hear what our body has been trying to whisper all along. Our body is always talking to us, sending us the messages that we need to hear, if only we would stop long enough to listen. We hold secrets in our own bodies. Each body holds the evidence of all that has gone wrong but it also holds the secrets, the wisdom and the mystery of how to let go and heal itself.

So please know that shame or fear or rejection don't have to be how things end. These things can actually be a beginning, as you dive in to discover where you hold them in your body. Choosing to let them melt.

You can actually choose to let go of the excess baggage you've been carrying and let it become part of what has made you into the beautiful soul you are.

You get to rewrite your own story, should you choose.

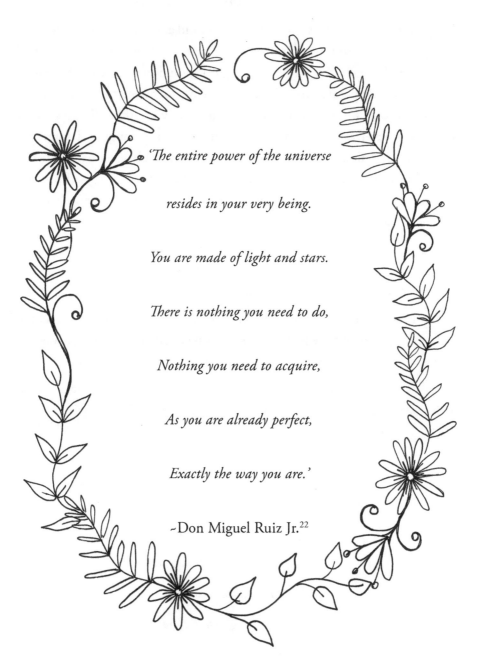

'The entire power of the universe

resides in your very being.

You are made of light and stars.

There is nothing you need to do,

Nothing you need to acquire,

As you are already perfect,

Exactly the way you are.'

~Don Miguel Ruiz Jr.[22]

CARVING OUT OUR OWN PATH

As a young teenager, I was just starting to unfold and emerge when suddenly being rejected meant my foundation of self-worth was demolished and replaced with shame. I did what I thought I should in an attempt to belong and it was a desperate struggle always trying to fit in, to avoid conflict and to succeed. Only now in my 50s can I fully see that all the striving and trying never actually earned me a true sense of belonging. I somehow always still felt alone. This constant striving only made it harder for me to really know my true colours. It caused me to leave parts of myself behind. It's only now that I am rediscovering those parts of myself that I had lost along the way.

My deepest fear of being hurt again had caused me to hide who I truly was. I had grown to believe that version of me was unlovable. Over time, I became so alienated from myself that even I forgot who I was.

As I have found the courage and guidance to dive into soul searching and healing work, I have had a series of awakenings. Discovering myself in a new way. Coming to value all of myself as I gain a new perspective.

I have learned that we invent our own beauty, we carve out our own paths. We sing our own songs and we are not alone while doing it.

'To heal means to "Make Whole"
and when we feel whole, we are
in touch with every part of us.
Our past, present and future self.
Embracing each part with love.
Fully accepting who we are,
Body, Mind and Spirit.'

Illustration by Mary Flora Hart

HEALING IS NEVER LINEAR

During my MFR journey, I began to see how I had spent years being uncomfortable in my own skin. I had been searching for myself in the world around me, instead of somewhere much closer to home. It hit me that I had spent so much of my life feeling displaced and estranged from my own body. It saddens me to know that for so long, I never fully inhabited the container of my life. I am grasping a new understanding, that in order to discover who I am, I have to climb inside the uncomfortableness of my own skin and I have to stay there long enough to truly discover myself.

When I began this work, I knew it would be hard, as I had spent so much time growing up consumed with thoughts of self-hatred and discomfort around how I looked and felt about my body. Maybe that's part of the reason I choose to escape and live life outside my body.

Exploring the darkness that lay inside, I could see my life reflected back to me in the many scattered fragments of who I was and who I ran the risk of becoming if I continued to ignore my body. I felt hollow, empty and had a profound sense of not belonging. Looking back now, I recognise this sad feeling of unbelonging had been present in my childhood and it had followed me into my adult life.

So I made the decision to enter into those dark places, to touch, feel and remember all that had created the darkness in the first place.

I can't quite explain how, but it felt like I was finding new parts of myself and with this came an ache to belong to my own body. I was learning not to hold back from the hurt or broken places, the wastelands, or the wounded depths. I began to see I could belong, that my body was becoming an enchanted place in which to fully dwell. I was becoming rooted in a newfound respect for just how amazing our bodies are and I was growing to care about my own body's health and integrity.

I started to realise that part of this unbelonging came not only from traumas but also from living life in the cages of culture, religion and expectations. Only now can I see that in order to fit in such cages, I was hiding parts of myself.

Surrendering to these cages imposed by culture was causing me to slowly die on the inside, losing sight of who I was created to be.

I began to explore and venture outside of these cages, only to discover a new way - that I owe my life to The Unseen, to the Beloved from which all things originate, that I wasn't on my own, that something much more amazing than I could even imagine existed right inside of me.

I began to feel suspended between the old version of myself and one I didn't yet know. I was moving towards fully accepting myself, able to look into my own eyes and not want to look away. The change was huge and it pulled me even deeper into a desire to become all that I was created to be.

LOOKING BACK

I kept looking back to see what else I could learn from my past. I was able to see how disliking myself for some reason came easily to me even as a child. It wasn't that I didn't feel loved, for my mum's love was very much visible and felt. But still, I felt I would never be clever enough, pretty enough, or enough to keep the love that was on offer to me. My sense of belonging, or lack thereof, obviously escalated to a whole new level when Dad left. I think that's when the self-hatred began to seep in. It's as if I forgot or couldn't see that I was loved.

As I became desperate for validation from others, I found myself stuck in a cycle of working hard and being a 'good girl.' Always making sure I was ticking all the right boxes. Doing exactly what society expected, despite the terrible feelings of failure and inadequacy that raged within.

I never took long enough to stop and breathe, to actually discover who I was and what I wanted from life. I was so consumed by trying to keep everyone else around me happy and proud of me that I didn't even know I had another choice. During those teenage years, in particular, the struggle to keep my head above water was all-consuming. So much so that I totally lost all sight of myself, becoming a carbon copy of who I thought everyone wanted me to be.

It was during this struggle that I grew so sensitive to any words or actions from others that I perceived as rejection or critical. My response was to retreat, internalising the criticism, letting it balloon out of control inside my head. And it was this downward spiral that caused my self-hatred to explode into loathing.

I remember one particular evening sitting around a fire pit with friends. I don't remember what triggered it, but it was like my body was there, but I was somewhere else, consumed by my thoughts. My mind was filled with darkness, stuck in a cycle of self-loathing, and feeling totally lost and alone, despite sitting around a fire with lots of friends. I suddenly realised there were tears streaming down my face, yet I felt nothing. I was numb.

It was dark and I remember lifting a small stone from the ground beside me. It had a sharp edge and as I sat there, I began to push it into the skin on my wrist, pushing and pulling it backwards and forwards across my wrist. I desperately wanted to feel something. How could I be surrounded by friends, by fun and laughter and yet feel nothing? I was surrounded but I'd never felt so alone. Slowly, I began to feel some pain pushing through the numbness, but I believed I deserved to feel this pain. I deserved to be punished. I was in a very sad and lonely place; my dad had chosen someone else to love. I believed I was no longer worthy of his love. My mum was in an even darker place as her whole life was falling apart. She had totally withdrawn and spent hours in bed crying or sleeping under the influence of sleeping pills to numb her pain.

It's only now looking back that I can see how all my feelings of inadequacy had smothered my joy. I was doing the best I knew how, and one of the ways I tried to cope was by always avoiding conflict for fear of someone disliking me or disagreeing with what I had to say. So instead, I shoved my words so deep inside me that I didn't even get to hear them form in my own mind. Not having a clear sense of self and worth, often left me immobilised and unable to stand up for myself. I avoided conflict like the plague.

Confrontation made me feel like I'd been swallowed whole and couldn't get back up for air. On some level it still does and even to this day, I tend to avoid conflict. My voice still shakes when I try to speak my truth aloud. I tend to automatically go to a place in my head where I'm the problem. Thinking it's all my fault that something is crumbling around me.

It has taken me almost 50 years to share these feelings of inadequacy and to begin to see myself in the reflection of my own eye when I look in the mirror. Only now can I look at my reflection in the mirror and say, 'I see you,' 'I've got you,' 'you're not alone,' 'thank you.'

Believe me, it has taken time and courage to journey within - to break through the armour and travel through the all-consuming darkness to find that spark of light that's been there all this time. Waiting to be found, waiting to be embraced, waiting to be nurtured back into belonging.

In fact, all of my life I've been waiting for someone to tell me that I am enough, when really, I just have to tell myself and choose to believe it.

MOVING FORWARDS

Still today, something can trigger that inner child in me, causing her to panic or even have a tantrum, with all those feelings I thought I had dealt with flooding back to consume me. It's like I revert back to being nine years old again.

I remind myself that it's ok. As we travel through life, we are always learning, always healing, we are all broken in our own ways. We can't run from it, it's part of who we are. Life is about learning to fall into our vulnerability, rather than ignoring it or hiding it. If only we can learn to accept ourselves, warts and all, then we might just learn to develop a new kind of resilience, remembering that magic can actually be found in the chaos and true healing can begin when we face our biggest fears.

During our time here on this earth, in this body, we might never reach an endpoint on our healing journey, but if we have the courage to walk this path, it will bring understanding and a learning to love who we are, as we continue to move forward.

It's taken a long time but eventually, I began to acknowledge and understand the role I have played in causing the way my life has turned out. But thankfully, where I am today is proof that we each have the power to mend ourselves. I'm not claiming to have it all perfectly worked out, but I'm moving forwards.

We can shift our story as we evolve and become more closely aligned with our soul's calling. As we embrace our inner child and bring them along with us for the ride, we can offer them explanation and comfort along the way, thanking them for helping to get you where you are today.

My desire is to not let my pain harden me but to stay soft and to keep showing up for myself, remembering that yes hurt happens, but so too does healing!

Life is a beautiful unfolding if we learn to let go and lean into change, rather than always tightening against it - embracing the newness and stepping out of our own way.

Change is clearly on the horizon, will you step towards building your dream, step out of your comfort zone and allow something new to take root? Always remember, we get to choose to foster life, rather than stamp it out.

Sometimes the way that we choose to live life keeps us small, as we focus on developing only certain parts of who we are. By doing this, our life gets squeezed into a shape that is not who we were created to be. It took me many years before I began to see that I was doing just this. But then it was like something deep inside became unlocked and started to seep through those long-lost parts of myself that I didn't even know existed. Something began to feed and nourish them.

Instead of concentrating only on the path before me, I started to heal the path within. Instead of searching for belonging outside, I began to understand that belonging already existed inside of myself, but first I had

'Follow your bliss and don't be afraid,

and doors will open

where you didn't know

they were going to be.'

~Joseph Campbell[23]

to learn to accept and love what I already carried within. I had to learn how to fully inhabit myself and love myself again.

The Covid pandemic in 2020 allowed me to slow down, causing me to find the opportunity to grow, creating a shift that has shaped my life from within. I was drawn to dwell even more deeply in my life, looking for belonging in a place I never thought to look before, grasping for something that I now know is within; it's the story of my Soul.

I felt compelled to write, which was funny in itself, as I was called dyslexic and illiterate at school by my English teacher. I could always see others' creativity and wisdom around me but by writing, I began to find myself. I began to forgive myself for doubting myself and putting myself down. There was something about writing my own story that gave me new sight. Writing has helped me to find a strength that had always been there, but that I could never quite see. It has helped me to understand that all my experiences, good and bad, can be used for growth. It has helped me to find my voice and get my power back, nudging me forward, step by step, on my journey of becoming, helping me to grow into who I needed to be.

'In the tapestry inside my head and heart,

a new weaving emerged

that made a kind of sense.'

~Lidia Yuknavitch[24]

Time

Time is our gift from the universe
With honour, grace and gratitude
being the only currency given here.

Nothing is for certain,
as I voyage through my vulnerability
Climbing each mountain with courage.
Time is my greatest teacher.

Teaching me how to be wiser
More tolerant, more forgiving.

Learning to open my hands,
to let go and to receive,
To embrace this body that carries me
To thank each part of me for
bringing me to where I am now.

Time has shown me
that learning to love myself is my greatest challenge.
Time reveals I am the creator of my own destiny.

Only with time can I begin to see
the armour I've worn for so long
Has been hiding me from the sunlight that
illuminates my authentic path
This armour has been hiding my voice
Keeping me small
Holding me captive

Only time can bring clarity,
perspective and a sense of peace
Creating space for change
As I find the courage to trust
That it's time to shed this armour

Becoming more transparent and curious
I walk forward to begin a healing journey
Knowing the path will not be linear

It's true the older we get the faster time goes
Fear rises, worried I won't have enough time
I bow down and relinquish control

Watching each season unfold
I am reminded time gives me
the opportunity for change
Learning to love more deeply
To allow myself to start over
as many times as I need to
Giving myself grace

I choose to celebrate this life
Honouring who I am
Using my voice

Accepting transformation is slow
I come to understand how
Building ritual is a sign of respect

Opening my mind and my heart
to what I knew but had forgotten
Focusing my attention on
what has fallen asleep in me
And sending my heartfelt thanks to the universe
For giving me the gift of time.

Part Two

CHAPTER SEVEN

Limiting Beliefs

UNWORTHINESS

When we find it hard to receive compliments, love, or attention it might be because we have a learned sense of unworthiness. Our unworthiness tends to act like a barrier against us being able to fully receive. This barrier can do so much damage, preventing us from opening up to the beauty that is all around us. Receiving a compliment is something I have always struggled with. It appears to bounce right back as I laugh it off and it makes me feel uncomfortable to be the focus of attention. It takes practice, like exercising a weak muscle, to learn how to embrace that beauty by accepting the compliments we receive.

Some of us have developed a lifelong habit of bracing against those moments when we are challenged to receive. Our awakening can be slow - like watching a slow-motion movie of a bud opening, growing and unfurling into life. But as we exercise this weak muscle, we too can begin to realise we have earned our place in this life as somewhere, somehow a deeper inner knowing is starting to bud. Only when our capacity to receive starts to expand do we realise how much of our life we have been spent constricted, limited and unseen. Only now can we even begin to invite light into those areas of pain and abandonment, with each compliment or act of love towards us starting to penetrate our thick skin.

I have always been a slow learner. At school, it took me hours to do what others did in minutes. But I always got there in the end. It's only now that I am learning to make a conscious choice to no longer brace against what is being offered and accept that it's ok to be seen.

Knowing that as I begin to thaw out those numbed parts of myself, it can be painful at first. A bit like that rush of blood back into a sleeping limb, causing those excruciating pins and needles. But I trust that, once I allow life to return and my emotions to flood to the surface, healing is taking place, healing of my body, mind and soul.

This journey can only begin when we learn to listen to our bodies; when we come into the stillness of our centre. It's here that we find our inner wisdom, guiding us to live the life of our dreams. A life that serves the world around us from a place of gratitude and well-being, as we travel along our own path towards healing.

I'm afraid a lot of my life has been spent achieving and pushing forward: giving, serving and repeat. I grasped at worthiness, never listening to my own body. I got so caught up in this vicious cycle that my body was crying out for rest, for grace and for some sort of slower rhythm, rather than the full speed ahead approach that I had become addicted to. Looking back now, it's not a bit of wonder my body got to the point when it dug its heels in and stopped at a dead halt after struggling for years with post-viral fatigue. I had run my body ragged.

But there was a light at the end of the tunnel. That light for me was the discovery of John F. Barnes Myofascial Release, which not only brought me total relief of my symptoms, but also started me down a totally new path in every conceivable way. It changed how I treated my patients and I found I was bringing them freedom from their symptoms. But this discovery also changed how I treat myself, how I live my life and has even inspired me to write this book.

Myofascial Release helped me to journey back to where my lack of worth was woven into my beliefs and into the very fabric of my body. After my dad left, as a 14-year-old, I obviously felt abandoned and unworthy. Over the following years, this belief became part of my DNA. Never changing, no matter what people told me and no matter how much I achieved in life. This resulted in some of my gifts being banished into the shadows of my unworthiness. If I perceived what I thought was a gift was being rejected or criticised by someone else, I would shove it so deep inside that over time I would forget it even existed. I became skilled at building up barriers in an attempt to protect myself from hurt. Only now some 40 years later, with the help of MFR and deepening my mind-body connection, have I grown to trust my need to take down those barriers so I might begin to allow my gifts to emerge from the shadows.

One such memory comes to mind when I was at school and my English teacher used to pick on me a lot, or at least that's what it felt like back then.

I was about 15 years old, and I hated reading aloud in class in front of all my classmates. I would always find myself so nervous that I would stutter and stammer my way through each paragraph. I now firmly believe I do have a form of dyslexia, but back then you were never assessed for such things.

On this particular day, my English teacher asked me to read aloud in front of the class again! As I struggled to string the words together, he totally lost his patience with me and shouted at me to sit down. He called me dyslexic and illiterate and told me that I would never amount to anything!

Still, to this very day, there are triggers that cause me to retreat into the shadows again - basically anything that makes me feel belittled, less than enough, humiliated, or left out. Any of these feelings will cause me to scuttle off behind my protective barriers and hide.

But at least I now have the understanding that I have a choice as to whether I stay there or whether I make slow incremental steps to reclaim who I was created to be from behind those barriers of rejection. It's been an uphill struggle but eventually, a gentle sense of worthiness has re-emerged.

Allowing me to become more whole. Causing the barriers to crumble and decay. I now realise that the mantra I had built my life around, 'I will never be good enough,' was a big fat lie!

I just have to be willing to acknowledge my triggers and choose not to hide behind the pain. I know that I often slip into a pattern of defensiveness and protection, causing my barriers to become once again physical in my body and resulting in me withdrawing from challenging situations. But I am continually trying instead to see myself with kindness and be willing to learn a new dance with the vulnerability that lies beneath.

By choosing to let my armour fall away and dissolve, I am allowing light to rush in from every side, allowing beauty to take the place of darkness, allowing the light that has always lived at my very core to re-inhabit each of the shadow places. This is subtly transforming the way I am doing life, clearing me out for something new. I am slowly learning to soften, honouring and even appreciating what I can learn from the unpleasant and the painful situations.

I am learning to open the doors of my heart to the unexpected explosions of light, to allow the fullness of life to sink into my very bones and to recognise what is teaching me to accept my gifts, even in the midst of suffering. Understanding that ups and downs are natural during the healing process, but I am compelled to continue to follow my bliss, offering my life back to that which gives me breath and letting joy live more fully in my life.

SELF-SABOTAGE

This journey of turning my gaze inward is helping me to unearth who I truly am. It is helping me to remove the weight of expectations I have placed on my shoulders. It is showing me that I don't have to remain small. It's like an awakening of something that has always been inside of me, hidden behind the armour. *I* built the armour and only *I* can take it down. I've allowed fear of failing to keep me small for far too long. I've lived my life surrounded by my invisible cocoon called fear.

Self-sabotage can take many forms. It can look like people-pleasing; comparison; perfection; holding onto past mistakes; control; suppressing emotions and not believing in your own worthiness.

What's on your list?

Self Sabotage causes you to shoot yourself in the foot.

Pain often causes us to self-sabotage, but it's up to us if we continue through life stuck in the cycle of self-doubt, or if we take courageous steps to get out of our own way.

It's important to note that doubt can act as a defence against our being rejected, causing us to continually avoid anything that takes us out of our comfort zone or challenges us. We tend to opt for whatever feels safe in order to avoid the risk of being rejected. But instead, perhaps we need to see doubt as an opportunity to choose to walk more bravely through our fears.

Doubt can, however, be so deeply ingrained in us, that it becomes like scar tissue, requiring us to make a conscious decision not to tighten and brace against our fear, but instead to soften and trust in our own mystery, taking up a new mantra as we step towards that which frightens us and looking out for the small miracles along the way.

Choosing not to disappear behind our armour of protection where we feel safe, choosing not to hold back and remain small, but instead to trust that each small thread you are stitching will eventually create something bigger and more beautiful than you could ever imagine.

On this journey, we can either choose to see fear, or we can see curiosity, intrigue and excitement. We can see vulnerability or instead we can choose to see courage. When we feel confused, accept that here in the confusion, we might actually find our very own creative expression. I know for certain this happened while writing this book when I hit a wall of confusion with two particular sections in this chapter. (Funnily enough one of those sections is titled "Self-Doubt"). It caused me to walk away and later return to write something better, with words from my heart.

When we feel resistance, know that it might show us a door to new possibilities. Believe me, I have felt a resistance grow about my writing. Who do I think I am, that I have anything to offer the world? But trusting in that whisper that draws me, compels me to write. I have opened new doors and completed my book which I only thought was a dream.

When insecurities flood us, learn that they might cause us to do things that make us feel empowered, finding courage in the doing. Pain might just encourage us to own our own story, to feel it and to create out of its power a story of feeling, healing and belonging. So instead of seeing things as obstacles, we can choose to explore each of our discomforts so that we might find the hidden gifts.

We can all begin this journey of finding our way back into our body, our most loyal friend. Each one of us can become more present to the life living inside of us. What do we have to lose by surrendering to the beauty that is inside each and every one of us, trying to unfold?

This journey has led me to a life of unfolding, bringing so much liberation, expansion and truth along the way.

SHAME

I grew up under a cloud of shame. The shame of thinking I was stupid, as I struggled academically at school with a much brighter sister. This struggle suddenly exploded inside my head, bringing me to a place where I felt it was impossible to achieve anything of value in my life. I grew up riddled with self-doubt, the shame of my parents' marriage coming to an end when I was 14, the shame of being chubby, never feeling slim enough or pretty enough. It only takes a tiny seed of shame and before you know it it has grown into a huge, deeply rooted belief that you're totally unlovable. This in turn, makes you feel unworthy of your own dreams.

I have had years of trying, striving and hustling for worthiness, but it wasn't until I began to look inside, really taking time to tune into my inner self, only then did I begin to actually learn that I could trust myself.

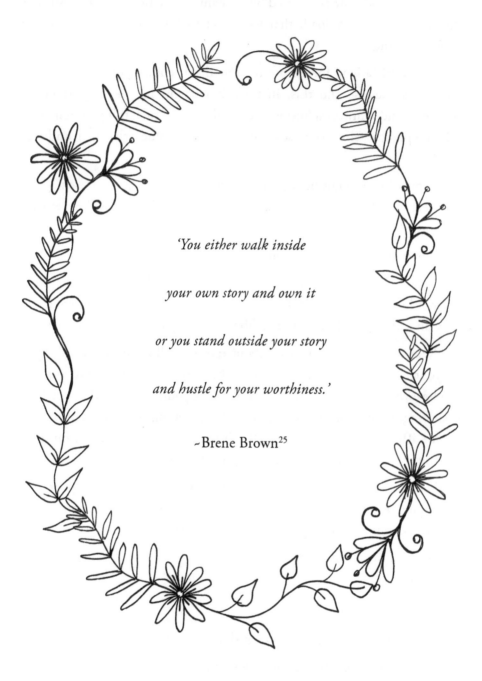

'You either walk inside

your own story and own it

or you stand outside your story

and hustle for your worthiness.'

~Brene Brown[25]

Our lives become consumed by so many distractions, worries, stresses, and information overload, that we forget to lean in and trust our own inner knowing.

Post-viral fatigue forced me to slow down enough to stumble across Myofascial Release and this, in turn, has taught me the importance of letting go and journeying inside. Here I discovered such things as self-trust, self-acceptance, self-esteem, self-confidence, self-value, self-worth and even self-love!

Some of you might be reading this thinking, that's a lot of 'self' going on there, but if we don't accept and love ourselves then we will never truly love others.

'Love your neighbour as yourself.'

I always struggled with that commandment as I knew I most definitely did not love myself. In fact, I probably spent more time hating myself. So, how on earth could I love my neighbour? Or anyone else for that matter.

Remember, self-love isn't all about ego. It is all about being willing to let yourself be loved - yes, by yourself, but also by those around you. You can love yourself in gentle ways, like allowing yourself to do what you love; exercising, walking in nature, or going for a massage or treatment of your choice. This grace you give yourself can have an uprooting effect on those negative beliefs you've been living with for too long.

You can learn to create affirmations in order to overwrite your self-sabotaging beliefs with positive ones. It may take years, but you can rewrite shame and victim thinking.

Some of my affirmations are:

I let go

I am worthy

I am comfortable in my own skin

Things are exactly as they are meant to be.

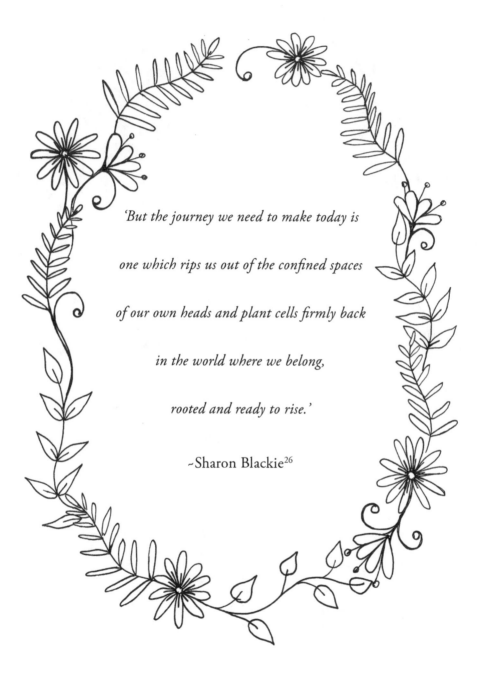

'But the journey we need to make today is

one which rips us out of the confined spaces

of our own heads and plant cells firmly back

in the world where we belong,

rooted and ready to rise.'

~Sharon Blackie[26]

Slowly but surely things will begin to shift, as you form new neural pathways. It's just taken me over 50 years to do it, but I did tell you I am a slow learner! However, I do now feel more comfortable in my own skin. I feel like I'm starting to love myself more fully, even though I see more wrinkles with each passing year and I am far from my lightest weight. But I can honestly look in the mirror and not have to look away with those judgemental self-hatred-filled thoughts that used to spiral out of control inside my head. I actually like what I see looking back at me. I don't start beating myself up but instead, I feel relaxed and at ease with myself. For far too long, I have forged a path through a dark forest of negativity and self-criticism, but now I feel I am rising up, rooted like a huge oak tree.

When shame is allowed to take root, it tends to flavour everything we do and say. The bitter taste tells us we are always wrong, inadequate and worthless. Shame is like a darkening shroud that wraps itself around our throat, silencing our sincerity and holding us captive. As we hide our shameful parts, we believe it will keep us safe from ridicule and harm. Little do we know this hiding comes at a hefty price, keeping us stuck, holding us back from discovering our own uniqueness.

Often the things we fight to hide reveal themselves as our magnificence if we choose to not stunt our growth. My shame of dyslexia and struggling academically could have stopped me from even attempting to write this book. Looking inside, I now understand that it took being rejected to make me see how I've been rejecting myself. It took me to acknowledge my brokenness to show me I can dare to be made whole.

Healing comes when we actually see all the broken parts of ourselves.

Instead of hiding them, try shining a light on those fractured pieces of yourself so you can retrieve the forgotten, neglected and rejected parts of your soul. By gathering all of these parts of myself into my arms, I can choose to carry them all to the other side of the pain, no longer keeping parts of myself hidden.

'And the day came,

when the risk

to remain tight

in a bud

was more painful

than the risk

it took

to blossom.'

~Anais Nin[27]

I have grown in courage as I learn that shame can't survive when we are willing to risk showing up for ourselves as fully as we are able to. Or when we reveal ourselves by being brave enough to step into the open and choose to trust not only ourselves, but others.

Trust makes us visible when we'd rather hide.

Trust allows us to ask for help when we feel abandoned.

Trust nudges us to drop our self-judgment and open up to vulnerability.

Trust prizes open the grip of shame, releasing us to more fully participate in life and all of its mysteries.

As shame began to lose its grip, I made choices to no longer shrink from my truth. To choose fulfillment instead of accepting to remain quiet. Yes, there will be a cost to stepping out into my purpose, but I know the price of remaining stuck would be even more intolerable.

I choose uniqueness over conformity,

I choose belonging over fitting in,

I choose wholeness over acceptance,

I choose awakening over shrinking,

I choose contribution over concealment,

I choose truth over silence.

I am choosing to write a new story.

SELF-DOUBT

Doubt is something we all struggle with from time to time. Looking back, I can see just how consumed my life was with self-doubt. I was like a fishing net, cast wide into a sea of doubt, catching every little doubt that could possibly exist as it floated by. Inside my head and my heart, I was overflowing with self-doubt. This made me afraid to be seen, afraid to be heard, never voicing my deepest thoughts.

Doubt is that story that plays out in our head on repeat, that doesn't end well. Doubt is the bitter juice we drink after we put equal quantities of rejection and criticism into the blender. Doubt is the scar tissue held in our body, carrying memories of our deep woundings. Doubt only serves to steal from us our ability to rise to a challenge.

Self-doubt can easily roll over into unworthiness. This unworthiness is often woven into our beliefs when we are wounded in earlier life. Many of us can look back to those key moments in life when someone's cruel words stopped us in our tracks and maybe even steered us in a different direction. When we feel unworthy it creates a barrier to receiving love from others. This is definitely still something I struggle with on a daily basis. Unworthiness also builds a barricade, behind which our gifts are hidden for fear of rejection or humiliation.

As I began to look inside myself, I discovered that I loved to write. But I had always just done so privately in my journals. Safe from the eyes of the world. I had chosen to believe the words spoken to me at school about being dyslexic and illiterate and amounting to nothing. I had allowed these words to steer myself away from my creativity, from relationships and from my gifts. But as I became more grounded in my body and in my life, something began to break through the barricade I had spent years constructing and it started to crumble. I became more open to meet life and to live it more fully.

So what if we choose to suspend our habitual pattern of allowing our doubt and fear to obscure our view of the world? And instead, treat new opportunities as the possibility for something amazing to happen?

Doubt can cause us to avoid, or doubt can ask us to step towards something frightening. If we can find the courage to reassure ourselves and meet it face on, just maybe a favourable outcome lies beyond our fear. Choose courage and believe in yourself, stepping into being seen, into

'With our shoulder always

to the wheel of life,

we can miss the very encounter

we've been preparing for.'

~Toko-pa Turner[28]

what you love. That's not to say that sometimes we might need to spend a little more time in our unreadiness. We all know that creation takes time. Ideas evolve, beginning to take shape and ripen during what appears on the surface to be a fallow time.

It's only when we look back that we can remember the grace it took as we allowed ourselves the time to dream and grow during a period where we thought we were hidden and stuck. Sometimes we are stopped in our tracks with illness or loss.

Covid-19 stopped me in my tracks as it did for most of the world. Lockdown was offering me an opportunity to become more attentive to my life. By being forced to slow down and becoming more present, I found myself becoming more porous to everything life had for me. Both the mystery and the magic. I felt a coaxing to not only put words down on paper, but to trust the dream of writing a book. At times it feels easier to hide my creative writing where it cannot be criticised, safe in the pages of my journal, where only I can see it, hidden from view. But I chose to listen when I felt a calling to journey on a new path, into a new purpose. Honouring what felt so out of reach somehow filled me with wonder and excitement. Stepping into this new openness has indeed allowed magic to happen. My greatest hope is that by drawing my story into the open for others and for me, that there is a chance that we can begin to live in alignment with our deepest calling.

There was plenty of time to plough the soil in which I began to gestate my dreams. Ideas, poems and words began to emerge, a creation I dreamed would serve others.

THE VOICE INSIDE YOUR HEAD

Why do we listen so intently to the voice inside our heads?

I don't know about you but 9 out of 10 times my voice is filled with negative comments about myself. Listening to this voice causes us to worry about what others think and ultimately drives us away from any chance of discovering our greatness. Moulding you into someone who really isn't you.

Listening to the voice inside my head I've begun to realise, I wouldn't talk to anyone else in the same critical and cruel way, even someone I really dislike. I am challenged to spend more time sitting next to my soul, to free myself from the tyranny of the voice inside my head. That voice that has been too loud for too long. What sort of life would I be able to live if I started to listen to the story of my soul or my true essence instead? As I drop into the well that lives inside me, I find a feeling of comfort - like I'm coming home.

We are all searching to find our way home back to our true self. But too often we get caught up searching for the answer outside of ourselves. When all along the answer lies deep inside. Always try to remember, just because we think it or hear that voice inside our head say it, it doesn't mean it's true. Instead, choose to live life out of your true soul space.

Something else that has helped me to quiet the noise inside my head is developing a mindfulness practice. This has enabled me to press the pause button and calm my emotions and thoughts. The more I have learned to pause, the more aware I have become of my body, and where I hold tension, worry, or stress. With this awareness comes choice. So as soon as I feel my body talking to me and telling me something isn't quite right, then it's up to me to choose whether I listen or not. And if I listen, what am I going to do about it? I have much more connection now between my mind and body and it feels good.

Through this process, I feel like I have found myself again and it has made me much more accepting and aware of my body. In some strange way, it's almost like I was totally living in my head, ignoring my body. It was almost an inconvenience having a body. Now, I feel more at home in my body and more grounded. It feels safe to be in my body as I continue learning more every day.

FEAR OF REJECTION

Even though I know my Dad did not intentionally reject me or mean to hurt or cause pain, rejection is something I experienced in my very bones. This rejection spiralled into shame. Shame demanded my silence, causing me to live withdrawn, dragging me down into despair, stopping me from fully participating in life. Fear of rejection was causing me to keep my writing where only I could see it, hidden from view.

The longer I carried that rejection with me, the more I imagined it being aimed at me every day, causing me to be ruled by fear, disconnection and shame. I began to ask myself, is this really the way I want to live my life?

Fear of rejection has wound its way through my story. But I can't blame it all on Dad's leaving, as I catch glimpses of it from an even younger age. It felt like I never truly fitted in and I have no idea where this feeling came from. I have so few memories from below the age of about 8. There are only snippets here and there. And in each of those earlier memories, I was always alone. I always felt like a spare part. It's only now that I am starting to feel like the rejected part of my soul just needs a little bit of admiration and encouragement and who knows what they might even produce with a little coaxing.

Somehow by acknowledging this deep-rooted fear, it is making me more open to all that life has to offer, the mystery and the expansion. Choosing to trust that magic can happen feels like it is helping to place me on the path of my purpose.

I realise I've been unconsciously telling myself this inner story of unworthiness and rejection from a very young age. Some of it has been influenced by authority figures whose words or actions have caused me to internalise the story I was telling myself.

I am not worthy.

I am thick.

I am dyslexic and illiterate and will amount to nothing.

I am not lovable.

This inner story runs deep and often affects the decisions we make, causing us to hang back or compare ourselves with others.

As I begin to write and read what I have written in my journals, I am enticed to dive deeper into the unconscious that has been carving out my path. It is here where I feel there is a crack of light being allowed to shine deep inside my soul for the first time, creating a welcome and unexpected encounter with my true self, my essence.

For so long, I have been swept along by the events of life that I have forgotten to stop and bring awareness to my dreams.

I am beginning to see that it is possible to alter the way I see my past.

By not only reconnecting with my dad after many years but also by connecting with each part of myself from my past and lovingly bringing them into the present, assuring them they are loved and needed on this journey. I am learning to become kinder to the "little me", by changing my inner dialogue, becoming more forgiving and nurturing as I lure her out of hiding and encourage her that she is very much needed to help me navigate this precious life, assuring them and myself, that our heart beats for us, that our breath breathes for us, and that we are all in this together.

We all have a choice to reframe each of those pivotal memories as an experience necessary in shaping us into who we are today. Even though the writing of this book some days feels insurmountable, on other days I am filled with adventure, learning, grasping, falling and getting back up again, relearning to let go and trust.

There have been so many different facets of learning and growing in my life especially over the last 6 years. Many of these are connected to traumas when growing up. My mind flits from here to there and back again, struggling with the order, planning and coherence. Having no idea how to put it all together but knowing deep inside my soul it will come together, somehow in the form of this book.

CHAPTER EIGHT

After The Rain

MISFIT

Despite spending most of my life striving to fit in, I have always had this deep knowing that I was created to do the opposite - to not fit in. This feeling came from deep inside. It felt like it was just the way I was wired.

The older I get, I realise I don't have to strive to fit in with the social and religious scripts that I have inherited along the way, scripts that tell us who to be and how to behave.

The only place I feel I did belong was with family, being a daughter, a wife, a sister, a mother. But outside of that, I struggle to fit in. For example with friendships, school, church and my culture, I always feel like I am on the outside looking in. Living on the periphery.

Growing up, I struggled with the education system. My confidence was destroyed, but somehow I worked out it was my hands I could offer.

At university, my assessors would always tell me I had great handling skills when practicing various techniques. I've always been much more comfortable with practical hands-on teaching than the theoretical or intellectual side of my work.

Life has taught me that while I might feel like I don't quite fit in, each of my vulnerabilities is potentially something beautiful. I've come to see that I have a voice that needs to be heard, I have a body worth listening to and that I have a story worthy of being told. Beauty doesn't always come from the expected. It can come from the strange, original and transformational parts of ourselves.

WOUNDS

Being an empath, for me, carries its dangers. I often find myself internalising other people's pain, becoming consumed by their misfortune, feeling helpless and drained before I realise that other people's pain and baggage aren't mine to carry. Only more recently am I beginning to learn to accept what I cannot change. I am trying to create more room in my mind for understanding what I can and can't control.

If only I could grasp the importance of letting go of my expectations of others, letting them be responsible for their own actions without getting caught up in trying to work things out in my head and trying to understand their decisions. What is actually important is my reaction to their situation. This acceptance of *what is*, is rooted in me doing my own personal work, especially when it comes to being in relationship with others.

After all, we are all broken people doing our best to live a life of joy.

I'm learning that in conflict, it's more important for me to be aware of how I am reacting as opposed to judging others or jumping to conclusions. When I am faced with conflict, my go-to is to withdraw.

I'm trying to learn how to speak up and express my truth and at the same time do my best to create space for acceptance and understanding, even when I'm feeling that I'm being rejected. This doesn't always go smoothly - it can feel like juggling too many balls all at the same time. But I do know that being silent doesn't resolve conflict or hurt feelings.

'Eventually we must take our life

into our arms and call it our own.

We must look at it squarely

with all its unbecoming qualities

and find a way to love it anyway.

Only from that complete embrace

can a life begin to grow

into what it is meant to become.'

~Toko-pa Turner[29]

As I try to cultivate a love that shows up even after disagreements or misunderstandings, I can see how this requires constant weeding of those toxic patterns I have developed in defense of the rejection and hurt experienced in my teenage years. As a teenager, conflict of any kind caused me to run in the opposite direction, putting my armour around my heart as I ran, causing me to detach and withdraw from the situation or even the relationship. I think, deep down, I felt like my heart would break and I wouldn't be able to put it back together again.

Over the years, becoming stuck in this pattern has undoubtedly cost me some friendships as I distanced myself by choice. So now I am trying to lean into my wounds in order to see what they continue to teach me, in the understanding that most of us all long for love, compassion and community. This pain from old wounds is something that always lingers. It is part of who we are. It becomes woven into the fabric of our being. Our stories are woven into the fascia of our bodies and they sit deep within our souls. Those wounds will always be there no matter how well they heal. A scar is a scar: ever-present. Perhaps it is there for a reason, to remind us of who we are. Becoming more self-aware will help us to see the weeds as they begin to sprout, so we can nip them in the bud before they become overgrown and tangled around our bones, causing feelings of regret to bloom again.

I acknowledge there will always be times or situations that trigger my pain and I can't ignore it or pretend it doesn't exist. In such times it's ok to feel it, to breathe even deeper into it and cry or scream. Indeed, it's vital to acknowledge our feelings and let them out in order to let it go.

Remember, it's never the goal to shove it down, ignore it or numb it. But rather to bring our awareness to it, wherever you feel it in your body, and to express it if you feel you need to.

This is all part of 'we have to feel, in order to heal'.

So it's important to find the balance between acknowledging the anger you might feel when someone triggers you and realising that right there and then might not be the appropriate time to let that anger out. Maybe you need to go home, scream into your pillow and then work out if a conversation still needs to happen with that person so that you can express your truth, rather than letting the unspoken things fester as you try to shove something down that needs to come out.

I remember encouraging one of my patients to do just this. This particular patient came to see me complaining of neck pain. Little did they know they were about to get rid of so much more than that.

During treatment, I was performing a cross-hand release over their chest area. This is a lovely technique that helps to open up the chest and the front of the shoulders, an area where so many of us tend to be tight. Our shoulders become rounded as we spend so much time sitting working at computers or just generally using our arms in front of us. Obviously, it is also the area of our heart where we often carry our heartaches.

3 to 4 minutes into this release, my patient's arms began to shake a little, so I encouraged them to keep letting go and to allow their body to do whatever they felt like it needed to do. The shaking intensified and spread to most of their body. The patient looked at me and asked "What's happening?" I explained their body was moving in order to get a better release of the fascia elsewhere. Their body was possibly processing trauma or emotions which had become blocked or stuck in the fascia. The body was trying to release what it no longer wanted to hold on to.

They then shared with me that it felt exactly like what happened to their body when they went through withdrawal during rehab for alcohol addiction. I explained that their body was remembering the trauma of this withdrawal and was trying to let go of it. They were happy to continue and as the movement gripping their body continued to intensify, their fists began to clench tightly as they began to thump the side of the treatment table. The patient could feel anger building inside. Anger perhaps with someone who had encouraged them to drink, anger maybe with themselves for all they had lost in their life, due to the grip this addiction had on every cell in their body. Who knows what this anger was about, but the important thing about this process of healing is that you don't have to work it all out, we just have to let go and let any emotions that flood to the surface, work their way out of where they have been trapped for too long.

After the treatment, I encouraged them to find a safe place where they could quiet down and continue feeling into their body. I advised them that if their body continued to shake, to allow it to shake and even to punch a pillow and give a voice to their anger, to make a noise, to allow those emotions to surface.

They reported complete resolution of their neck pain, but hopefully, they also learned a lot more about their body and how to release all that no longer serves them.

We are all worthy of forgiveness, so love yourself enough to mend what has been broken and to tend to what is hurting. You are braver than you imagine and more resilient than you will ever know. It's only when we choose to forgive others and ourselves that we can catch glimpses of our true potential. Knowing that we all fall short, we all make mistakes. Knowing we don't have to carry the rejection, the self-judgment, our past, the unworthiness. We can unpack our baggage and we can choose to leave it behind as we continue on our journey.

Maybe then we can begin to trust we are worthy and grasp that we have a say in what comes with us on our journey. We can choose to be gentle with ourselves. Giving ourselves grace and permission to create a new path. We are always a work in progress.

We can always find new strength embedded in our obstacles.

Let love seep into your bones and dissolve your armour.

Place your hand on your heart and say to yourself,

'I love you,'

'I'm listening.'

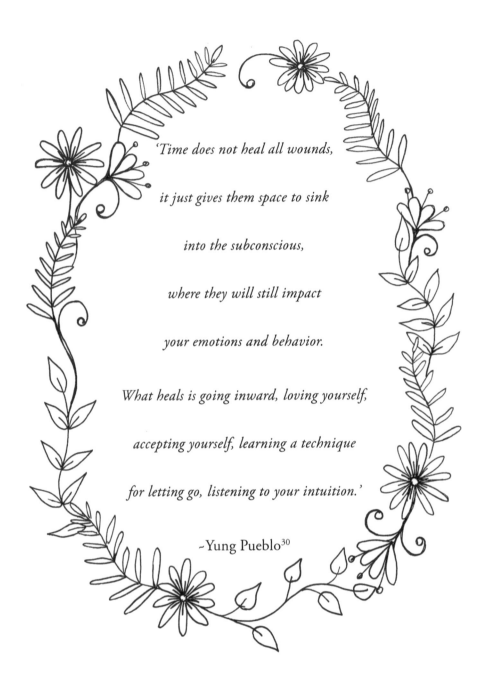

'Time does not heal all wounds,

it just gives them space to sink

into the subconscious,

where they will still impact

your emotions and behavior.

What heals is going inward, loving yourself,

accepting yourself, learning a technique

for letting go, listening to your intuition.'

~Yung Pueblo[30]

SOUL WORK

My heart's desire is to live a life of purpose, larger than I can begin to imagine. But so often the echo of my past stories pulls me back into old patterns of stuckness. It has taken me many years to pluck up the courage to inhabit those shadow parts of myself, where I've been forced to relive the pain, the trauma, the rejection and the loss. But by this exploring, I get to choose to break the pattern of staying tight and defensive and instead to unfold and open into belonging.

I don't know about you but some days I feel like a child trapped inside a woman's body and on other days I feel like a woman nurturing her inner child. I am reminded that it takes a whole human being to find their right path. So, I embrace the inner child and the woman I am today, as well as all the other parts of me that have journeyed in this body over the years.

If I remain fractured into many pieces, I will never find my way home.

I can't ignore any one part of myself if I hope to live a fulfilled life. It requires that I take all of me, my mind, my body, my emotions and my spirit, along for the ride.

As we all know, growth can be painful. It requires our full attention and asks that we show up fully for ourselves. All too often our past still causes us pain, but without it, we wouldn't find our light. All of our past experiences, good and bad have shaped us into the person we are today.

There comes a time when we have to stop blaming outside sources for our loss, lack, pain, or misfortune and instead take accountability for our own choices. Realising we have the power to set the course for our own life.

We can rewrite our story.

We can choose a different path.

We can find a different narrative to live by.

We can be distracted by lies, by negative voices, be they internal or external voices. Or we can find our own truth and step into our own power, trusting our very own path. I know this is far from easy but learning to trust myself has been one of the most challenging and rewarding things I have done as I journey towards becoming who I was told I would never be. By choosing to see myself as worthy, I am catching glimpses of who I really am and who I want to become.

Change, however, requires us to embrace the shift, instead of opting for what feels more familiar and safe. So often we run away from the unfamiliar, preferring to hide in what is comfortable. But this can turn out to be unhealthy as it continues to make us feel unworthy of authentic change. I am trusting that as self-belief increases, fear will lose its grip. That by facing my biggest fears, I am allowing healing to flow, giving me the courage to become who I want to be.

Sometimes it's not easy to understand what is going on inside our heads. But maybe if we listen, really listen, with our whole heart and our whole body, we might just be able to clear a gentle space for our thoughts and feelings to land, so they can begin to make sense. It can feel terrifying, but it can help us begin to work things out, rather than shoving it down and ignoring what our soul is trying to say.

Sometimes we have to dive even deeper into our vulnerabilities and flaws in order to find our truest self, so that we can bring her into belonging. This deep diving has taught me to have compassion for my past and the people in it, to let go of judgment and not to point the finger of blame.

Some of our stories remain unspoken and that's ok, but the more light we can shine into those stories, the less hold they have over us and the freer we become to live our lives full of joy.

All of this soul work has shown me that each and every one of us is born worthy! But, unfortunately, life teaches us to search for worth or to prove our value. We become blinded to the beauty of our beingness. We lose the sense of knowing and feeling that we are already abundant. We no longer feel in our bones that we are enough.

Perhaps it's time to find a different way, to recognise our story needs to change, finding a new paradigm for what it means to be human. This new story might just reveal to us the greatest treasure of all.

There comes a point when we become exhausted from all that searching and striving for worth. If only we had listened to those ancient rumblings from deep within, that tell us to stop searching for what is already there, deep in the marrow of our bones. Bone marrow has everything it needs to carry oxygen, fight infection and stop bleeding. It is essential for life. Just like each one of us has exactly what we need, it is crystallized deep in our very bone marrow - we just need to let it flow. Trusting our own voice, knowing that each one of us has our own unique expression:

It will bring healing.

It will bring joy.

It will bring hope.

Let it go and let it flow.

Trust yourself.

Feel the power of your dreams.

Soul's Quest

As I begin to listen to my body
Something cracks open deep inside.
I begin to hear my soul.

As I rediscover my body
Feeling safe enough to climb back inside
I discover my essence.

She is soft, she is tender
She moves like liquid
When I let go.

All along she has been hiding under the surface
Dwelling in the shallow waters of my being.

She longs to be held gently in my heart
Love is her language
Always available when I ask for help
She swaddles me in unconditional love.

Pure and wise she lives in my greatest depth
I have the power to call her into form.

She is present
She serves
She heals
She replenishes and restores
She is love.

As I learn to drop inside
I feel rooted in her presence
Her softness can be felt in my breath.

When I rest, I can feel her peace
Each time I return
She sets me free.

Choosing to stop tightening and bracing against life
I have found her comforting touch
As I learn to speak a new language to my body
One of well-being
One of restoration
One of grace.

I am breathing the soft one within me awake
As I listen to her message
I am learning to listen to my soul.

CONFESSION

So, I have a confession!

I definitely have an addiction to nice things. When I see something beautiful online or in a shop, I want to have it. I want to wear it, thinking it will make me feel good about myself. And it does, the first time I wear it. So I get a little bit of a high, but it only lasts until I see something else that looks even more beautiful.

I know this addiction is a sign of a deeper need. A need to be seen, to be loved. I guess my addictions are an attempt to meet my subconscious need for validation and belonging. But perhaps the even deeper need is that I need to look in the mirror and really see myself, not just the beautiful clothes I'm wearing. I want to love myself. I want to feel alive. Interestingly, when you actually start to like yourself, you no longer need all the things you thought you needed to be happy in the first place.

So I've decided to try something new. A little experiment. I've decided to sit cross-legged in front of my bedroom mirror every morning and look into my eyes. Not the way you look into the mirror when you're getting dressed or doing your makeup in the morning but to really look into my own eyes and hold the gaze. To look beneath my skin. I will try to hold my own gaze and not look away.

'There she is, that's me!'

Why is this simple exercise so hard? Why is my mind so predisposed to negativity? I am constantly talking to myself and I don't know about you but 99% of what I say to myself is negative, self-critical and downright cruel.

Interestingly, however, when I look into my dog Milo's eyes, I am filled with loving thoughts and words. Telling him how handsome he is, how he's gorgeous and I love him. He soaks up every word and snuggles in closer, returning the love I give him.

So as I look into my own eyes again, I try to see the parts of me that I can love:

The two-year-old me, sitting in a Silver Cross pram at the front of my home, alone.

The five-year-old me playing with my older sister and her friend. Play-acting with me being the abandoned baby they find on the doorstep. Fussing over me and showering me with love and attention for 2 minutes before putting me to sleep in a cot, so that they can continue with their acting as Charlie's Angels.

The nine-year-old me diving for cover when the bomb went off on our front doorstep, petrified and heart racing with fear.

The 13-year-old me being forced to read out loud in front of the whole class. My English teacher, shouting at me telling me I'm dyslexic, illiterate and will amount to nothing.

The 14-year-old me, who's world has just fallen apart after being abandoned for real when my dad leaves home and does not come back.

The 22-year-old me, who's just had a tumour removed from the roof of her mouth being told it was precancerous.

The 27-year-old me who's just given birth to a 9-pound baby boy, loving him to bits but struggling with postnatal depression.

And yet I survived.

And I thank each one of these parts of me for all they have done to get me to where I am today.

I look deeper into my eyes in the mirror and I smile a little. I see parts of myself that are kind, parts that are courageous and brave, parts that are caring and yes even parts that are beautiful.

I begin to accept that I am a multifaceted spiritual being.

That I need to love and be kind to myself.

I need to accept, care for and see the beauty within myself.

Realising I have everything I need and nothing has been wasted.

My entire past is holding me up and has made me who I am today.

I am always going to be me, I need me to survive. To live and to fulfill my purpose right here in this life.

This is where I belong.

Here in this human body that is looking back at me from the mirror.

I am slowly learning to depend on the voice of inner wisdom instead of the voices of outer approval.

It's as if the old me doesn't like what she sees in the mirror, because she sees the negative that others have put on her. The old me isn't enough unless she works hard, dresses perfectly, straightens her hair, or loses weight. I feel strangely suspended between this old version of me and the one I don't yet know. But the version of me that I don't quite know yet, wants so desperately for me to fully accept and love myself. To discover the diamond within.

As I dig deeper, I know if I can't validate and love myself unconditionally no matter what other people think of me, even if I don't succeed, even if I don't look cute in my clothes, then I will never experience the true freedom I was born with. This conditioning that compels me to succeed and have nice things runs deep. So when I feel lazy, I tell myself I'm not being productive, or when I feel that I don't look cute in a nice outfit, I step towards that slippery slope of self-loathing again. But now I am choosing to change the voices inside my head to say to myself, I love you and I always will. You are perfect just as you are. I have for so long chosen to remain small, to be the victim, to be invisible, simply because it felt safer.

But I am trying to step out of powerlessness, hopelessness and victimhood. Stepping away from these things and stepping into my personal power. Step-by-step I will grow, I will change, I will be transformed and I will be strong and grounded in myself and in my body. We are each mind, body and soul, interconnected and whole.

Then, maybe I can hear myself even a little bit. Maybe I will realise I can't fill the gaping hole of validation and self-love with possessions and

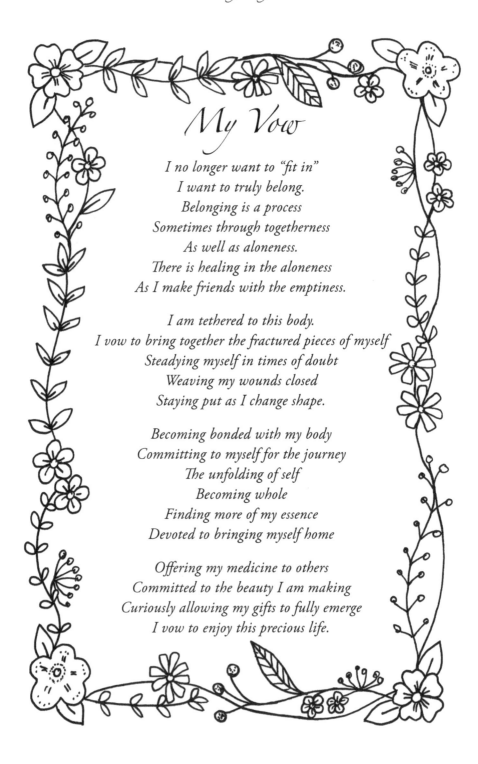

My Vow

I no longer want to "fit in"
I want to truly belong.
Belonging is a process
Sometimes through togetherness
As well as aloneness.
There is healing in the aloneness
As I make friends with the emptiness.

I am tethered to this body.
I vow to bring together the fractured pieces of myself
Steadying myself in times of doubt
Weaving my wounds closed
Staying put as I change shape.

Becoming bonded with my body
Committing to myself for the journey
The unfolding of self
Becoming whole
Finding more of my essence
Devoted to bringing myself home

Offering my medicine to others
Committed to the beauty I am making
Curiously allowing my gifts to fully emerge
I vow to enjoy this precious life.

achievements. Instead, I can fill this hole by learning to love myself as I am. I long to know my essence, and to grasp that my soul is perfect just as she is.

SYNCHRONICITIES

Sometimes when we commit to something that we know is going to stretch us, we start to feel increased areas of tension in our body. I know for me I become aware of clenching my teeth in bed at night, which then causes severe neck tension and headaches to build. For example, when I said out loud that I was going to write this book, I could feel the pressure building in my body. But I had to choose to trust myself and who I was becoming. There were little synchronicities and some not-so-little ones, like Covid-19 causing a worldwide lockdown, which gave me the time to slow down and realise there was more than just words in my journals, that just maybe there were the bones of a book.

Then at exactly the same time a friend, Deb, from Sedona, just happened to be starting a coaching course online. It was a 10-month programme called Artists in Action Conscious Creativity. One month prior to Deb starting this course, I would never even have contemplated me writing a book. Sure, I had journaled over the years and enjoyed it, feeling it was my form of meditation, my way to commune with the Divine, to experience true connection. My journaling feels sacred, spiritual, it offers me sanctuary.

Instead of feeling totally out of my depth and falling into the trap of comparison, where I always come up short, I chose to connect to what I truly felt I was being called to do. I decided that if, in writing this book, there was a chance to connect with someone and have an impact on their life, then I would jump in with both feet and do it. I began to enjoy the process, even though I really hadn't a clue where to begin. I found that as I wrote and developed this new skill, it helped me process and learn. It became a passion, as I felt a new form of creativity flood into my life.

Perhaps writing is a passion I've always had, but it was hidden under the weight of unworthiness because it had been rejected or humiliated in the past. I had shoved it under this barrier as it made me feel safe and protected for a time. But for some reason, it now wanted to come back into belonging with me.

My journaling has helped me to unstitch the threads of fear and darkness that are woven into my tissues. As I begin to listen, I'm guided by an inner voice showing me the truth underneath it all.

Learning that our internal landscape is the home of our healing, writing has allowed me to meet myself with love, honour and gratitude.

It has revealed the part of me that is source - the source I was born as and from.

I've discovered my light that whispers over and through me with love and grace. It has led me here. It has brought me home.

OBEDIENT OR WILD

For most of my life, I've only been able to see two possible paths, obedient or wild. Of course, I opted for the obedient path. It was all part of my plan to fit in and be good. But now I'm realising it's healthier to acknowledge our shadows and to accept no one is all light. We all have light and darkness in us.

It's only when we acknowledge that shadows exist, that we can hope to stop them from expressing themselves destructively. This expression can be internally or externally. My shadows tend to be expressed mostly internally. In patterns of self-hatred and deep shame. Choosing to believe I was never enough. Never good enough, never pretty enough, never clever enough. It was like something was always missing. My chosen patterns of behaviour created an insatiable hunger to be loved, to belong, to be valued, to be worthy. This was my driving force, pushing me to achieve and to accomplish. All in an attempt to win me approval from others. And yet the only thing this driving created were areas of desertion within. I was the one abandoning parts of myself. I was the one doing the rejecting.

It wasn't until I discovered MFR that I found a way to go directly to the root of the damage. Layer-by-layer I'm bringing myself back into belonging, revealing the gifts and abilities I already possess. Now I am travelling the path that helps me to fully accept my flaws and my oddities as part of my wholeness. I am learning that it's ok to allow a little bit of the wild me to express herself by getting a tattoo or two. I am learning to show up fully, reclaiming the parts of myself that are afraid of being hurt or left behind. By learning to include all my parts, I have found my way home to belonging, fully accepting that everything belongs.

Bringing Myself Home

I never knew I was allowed
To feel my deepest heartache
To feel my deepest fears

Instead, I ignored my feelings
I abandoned my own body
I left the seat of my heart

As I begin to thaw my frozen emotions
I am learning to find my voice
Listening to my needs and finally finding freedom

I enter the grace my body offers
Becoming more receptive to my spirit,
My heart, myself.

No longer denying who I really am
I am bringing myself home
Becoming who I was born to be

Open to my feelings becoming part of me
No longer disconnected from my tender heart
No longer living in fear of my emotions
But giving them a place and a voice

Without shame or embarrassment
Fostering peace and love on the inside
Allowing myself to come home.

CHAPTER NINE

Bumps Along The Way

THE INVITATION OF PAIN

Of course, there have been bumps along the way. In November 2018, I tore a disc in my lower back. Not only was I in excruciating pain, but I was embarrassed. Me, a Physiotherapist, finding myself in this situation and I couldn't fix it. How incompetent of me, I specialised in the treatment of Back Pain and had done so for over 15-years. It seemed like the ultimate irony, that somehow I was suddenly transformed from the master of a problem to its grovelling victim.

I threw everything I could think of at it, pushing my agenda on it, but it still held a tight grip, consuming me with pain. My struggle to get on top of it only resulted in me falling deeper into the pit. I felt as if I was being buried alive. It wasn't until I stopped all the striving and pushing to fix myself, until I let go of the outcome, until I became willing to walk with the pain that it reduced dramatically overnight. It was like a surrendering, an acceptance, that this too belongs.

This was not a quick process - it took over 15 weeks to get to this point. I have always said I'm not a quick learner. It's only now looking back that I can see how I immediately fell back into my old pattern of "pushing through", becoming fixated on eradicating the pain. Meanwhile, this pain was actually trying to teach me something. There was a deep humbling taking place as I was brought down onto my knees. I was learning a willingness to dance with the unexpected in life.

I was letting go of the need to arrive and leaning into being present with what is. I know deep down that often pain comes to break us open in order to create something bigger, something more beautiful and something more full of love.

Even with all my new learnings and insights, life can still lead you off your path. Life has many twists and turns along its complicated winding path as your journey unfolds. But I remind myself of how I have found my new path and how I have embarked on a new journey, one which helps to make sense of the old. I cling to this new path as it brings me closer to my truth and shows me what nourishes and empowers me.

That's not to say it doesn't take monumental efforts to stay on this path. There are times I grow tired and jaded, but the choice is mine to rise up and follow this new way to live. I have to remind myself often to detach from who I once was in order to truly discover who I am meant to be. It is hard, and sometimes I fall forward stumbling into the unknown, but it's often rewarded with finding my way to that deeper knowing that now I am on the right path.

COURAGE TO STEP OFF THE EDGE.

Imagine a beautiful birdcage, where a bird enjoys living life feeling safe and secure. So often we opt for living life from somewhere that feels safe and secure for us. It's here where the temptation to stay withdrawn from a challenging everyday world can be strong. But the chances are that sooner or later the world will come knocking on the door of our cage. We have to take flight to really gain an understanding of our place in the wider web of life

on this beautiful and mysterious earth. With that leap into the unknown, we find freedom, we find transformation, new insights and strengths are uncovered. We miss out on so much by remaining in the safety of our cage. We miss out on finding a place where our particular gifts and wisdom can flourish. A place from which we can speak. A place to truly belong.

We swaddle ourselves so tightly, retreating inside our own heads looking for the solutions to all our problems in the centrality of our own self.

I wish I could go back in time and realise that the world wouldn't stop spinning if I actually spoke my mind, opened my mouth, stood up and walked across a crowded room, or got a tattoo.

Only now do I believe that I deserve to take up space on this planet.

Only now do I see that fear doesn't own me.

Only now do I fully accept myself as someone who is human and honest, messy and truth-telling, giving myself permission to be fully me.

When we try to control something, we can't fully listen. So when we try to control our bodies, we can't truly understand the wisdom they contain.

Yes, listening can hurt, we tend to numb it so we don't have to attend to it, when really we owe our bodies so much credit for all they do for us. Our bodies are far wiser than we give them credit for. Maybe it's time to start listening to the wisdom that lies within. When we get out of our own way and open up to all that is around us, nature, mystery, divine essence, often we uncover the nature of our true work, embodying our sense of deep belonging, crashing headlong into its arms. That's not to say that sometimes we mightn't walk in storms so fierce that we can hardly stand up. But know you will survive. Keep whispering your hopes and dreams as you place one foot in front of the other until you take flight again, as you come out the other side of the storm and into the light.

As I share this experience of one of my MFR treatments, I share it only to give you the courage to step off the edge and into the darkness, as sometimes this is necessary to let the light in.

As I lay on the treatment table, my body started to unwind. My hands were clamped on either side of my head covering my eyes. It was so dark and scary, with increasing pressure inside my head. It felt like my head would explode as the pressure and darkness built, like I was pushing my head through solid rock. Of course, my brain kicked in and I started to think, maybe I was in a tunnel, or was it a birth canal? Slipping down into the silent dark womb of the Earth. I tried to remind myself that I didn't have to work it out and just to trust the process.

All I knew was that I somehow felt safe, even though the darkness was so complete that it felt tangible. I felt somehow protected. I felt called, in that moment, to stay with the healing that lay in this darkness. I knew that any moment I could open my eyes and be in the treatment room again with my therapist. I knew I could find my way back out of the dark.

Staying felt safe and it felt terrifying all at the same time. It was like I could hear the Earth breathing, calling me to stay. It felt like I was at a portal to an entirely unfathomable world, just hidden from view. This gateway leads to possible transformation, a deep and enduring transformation should I choose to trust what my body was doing.

This experience could catapult me into a new way of seeing, a new way of being in the world. I would learn that each and every unwinding was a source of transformation, wisdom and inspiration, should I trust enough to let go. My body had the ability to let the therapist into the secret places, the places I didn't even know existed, let alone that they held such darkness. Sometimes it takes courage to step off the edge. It feels like you are losing your footing, plummeting down into the darkness. Scream if you need to, but let yourself fall and let yourself sink to the bottom and in doing so it might help destroy old ways of thinking and help to remove limiting beliefs. All this might just prepare us to develop the wisdom we need to give birth to our most authentic self. The self that can begin to act from a place of solid grounded rootedness.

This journey has required me to sacrifice the parts of me that keep me stuck in my own wasteland. Sometimes we need to be taken apart and broken into pieces so that we can begin the process of putting the fragments back together again. Searching for the lost pieces of ourselves that we need so that we can start to knit ourselves together, rebirthing into a new pattern.

Inside those old stories there are whispers, trying to call us back into the old patterns of existence. But if we have the courage to keep nudging forward, knowing that it's ok to let ourselves break open, to express our rage, to step over the threshold into the darkness, we can trust that the gifts we receive will be more than worth the journey.

Learning to let go and going with the flow of our body allows transformation. It can even feel a bit like we are shape-shifting as we learn a new way of being. We stand taller and become more at ease in our own skin, with a stronger sense of belonging.

It was necessary to dive deep into myself so that I might discover what it was that I needed to lose before I could see a glimpse of what I might become. In staying with the darkness, I gathered the strength I needed to find a way back to my path and to face the rest of the journey ahead.

As I step into this age and stage of life, I am choosing to let go of the fear and the shame that has coloured most of my life with shades of grey. Instead, I am stepping into my power and telling the stories that need to be told. I am learning to surrender to something bigger and stronger than myself. I am finding clarity as I write to harvest all that I have learned from my story. I am feeling compelled to share with my feet planted and a true sense of rootedness.

I am remaining open to new wisdom yet to be learned from this body as I continue to shrug off all that no longer matters. I am free from the old shackles that used to confine me and consume all my energies.

I am finding freedom from the need to constantly accomplish and instead, realising the slow dawning of a passion to create what burns in my heart.

Called To Courage

I am walking a path
Through a pathless forest
Each step marks
Where I am going
And where I have been

Telling my story
Finding my voice
Each word showing the way
Trees with their outstretched arms
Keeping me safe as I pass by
Accompanied by the softest of rain

Looking for the right path
I come to a bridge
Covered thick with moss
This is where it begins
Will I cross this threshold?
Set out on a pilgrimage?

Following the mystical golden thread
I can see before me a Labyrinth
A vision that I long for
That inspires me and draws me forward

I take a step onto the bridge
Feeling the soft earth beneath my feet
I set off on a quest to find my way
To forge my own path

Emerging out of the darkness
Begins with those first hesitant stumbling steps
Stepping into transformation
Searching for the lost pieces of myself
Knitting them together in my heart

Breaking through what I perceive
To be my own limitations
Uncovering both my weaknesses and my strengths
I begin to recover an understanding
Of my own place in the world

Walking my own way back into being
The path will vanish behind me
As I emerge into the light

Each written word will help me
To hold on to the learning
To see the gifts imparted along the way
As I walk the path called "Courage"
I begin to dance.

STEPPING INTO YOUR GREATNESS

Recently I feel that I hold my greatness in my throat, not letting it escape up through my vocal cords and out into the world.

But by suppressing these words, my voice, I am suppressing my greatness. By recognising my voice, my words, my writing as part of my greatness, I feel like I've come home to myself. I've found where I belong. This part of me makes me more complete. When I tap into and recognise this greatness in myself, I am becoming a truer more complete version of myself. Even though sometimes:

I don't want to live life any longer with a limited palette of colours. I want to let go and allow my greatness to direct and shape my life into what it is meant to be.

No longer safeguarding myself against vulnerability.

No longer held captive by my silence.

No longer allowing the fear of criticism to prevent me from releasing something beautiful into the world.

'the cost of stepping into your bigness is

high, but the price of remaining small is

intolerable'.

~Toko-pa Turner[31]

CHAPTER TEN

Writing Myself

Into Freedom

THE RIGHT TO BE A WRITER

I've been journaling for years and years, since somewhere in my early teens. It has always felt like a safe place, where I have permission to be me. I've often felt that my words sound better written than they do when they come out of my mouth. When I journal, I find myself in a sacred place, a place where thoughts can become crystallised, a place my writing is unedited but authentic.

It's like sitting down with an old friend and becoming fully present with no distractions, able to be my entire self with no filter. My journal is always there for me, offering me a safe place to be vulnerable without the fear of judgment. Writing allows me to smile on the inside, giving me permission to stretch and grow. It has enabled me to begin to believe in myself, as I choose to let go of doubt and accept that I am enough.

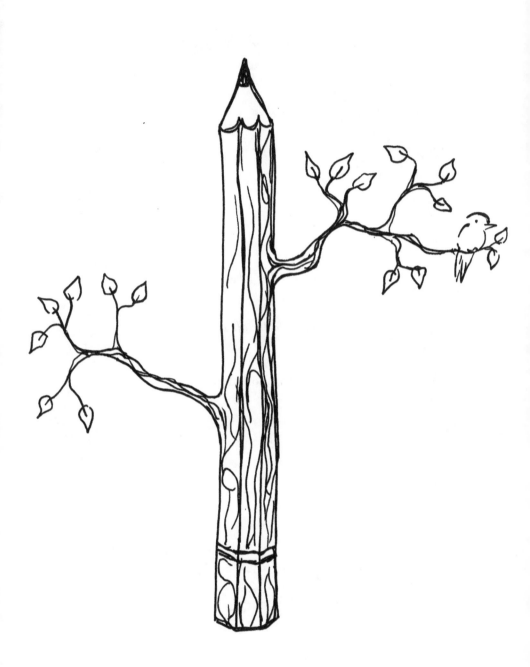

'Shame dies when stories

are told in safe places'

~Ann Voskamp[32]

As I've shared, growing up I often felt I was never complete or enough. Always searching for and striving for acceptance. I spent years searching but didn't quite know what I was looking for. I know now it was all those missing parts of myself, parts that I've only grown to know in recent years. Initially, I chose to live life from the safety of my comfort zone, preferring not to be seen or heard. I was stuck in these old patterns for so long that I became accustomed to and comfortable with hiding in the shadows. I didn't know there was a choice to break out of this mould. So instead I did what was expected, by shrinking into the world around me.

More than 50 years of keeping quiet and toeing the line had caused me to lose my voice. Maybe that's why to this day I still hate the sound of my own voice. But now I am beginning to understand how my experiences have guided me into writing. It's a huge part of my creative expression. I feel like the little girl who felt so lost, is now the little girl who I have found inside who helps me write. The more I write the more I understand that my traumas, bombings, abandonment, depression are places of storytelling. As I learn to trust myself, to give myself permission to use my voice in new ways, I am accepting it's not up to others to make me feel complete or enough, only I can do that! Writing about my journey is helping me to explore changes with intention. Writing is giving me space, time and the creativity to mark this passage more deeply. To be able to express the conscious and unconscious layers of my unfolding.

My deepest desire and dream is to write words that share wisdom, bring healing and give inspiration to others on this journey.

What if I've been chosen to write this book, to tell my story?

INVITING PRESENCE

My writing ritual was helping me to invite presence into my everyday life, to centre myself. Somehow by inviting this presence, I was becoming more porous to the mystery life has to offer.

'Are you going to go on the creative Soul's

quest or are you going to pursue the life that

only gives you security?'

~Phil Cousineau[33]

Maybe, as I pluck up the courage to visit each of the shadow parts of myself...

Doubt

Fear

Rejection

Shame

Self-criticism

Pain

Sorrow

Loss/ grief

Anger

Restlessness

Impatience

...just maybe, I might find out what they are trying to teach me. I might discover a new purpose, a new dream might just unfold. I might even be able to grow and become more at home in my own body.

This inner work requires time and presence.

I was beginning to see how so much of my life had been spent armouring myself in an attempt to protect myself from rejection, pain and loss. When all along, the armour I had created, just kept these fears and doubts embedded deep in my very core, each one controlling a huge part of who I was becoming. Indeed, holding onto these shadows had caused my insides to become cold, dark and inhospitable to myself and others around me. I knew for certain I wanted to try to cultivate an inner hospitality, where life would be welcome to enter and fully inhabit.

If I could more fully live in my own body and make it my home, then maybe the magic and mystery of life would feel welcome to join in.

Little did I know that opening the door of my heart and welcoming life to weave itself more fully into the fabric of my body would create such a sense of true belonging. This process only began to happen when I started to let down the walls I had built, initially there for protection. But I somehow got so used to the armour-plated walls being there that I believed I needed them to protect my vulnerable parts.

I became too afraid to look behind the armour, in case I didn't like what I saw. With time, I realised that by starting to allow the light into those darker parts of myself, I was beginning to allow my armour to melt away. I was creating a place of beauty that I could be proud to call home, creating a welcoming presence that enables me to communicate more clearly, creating belief, trust, contentment and grace, with a deeper understanding that I am moving in the right direction.

This inward journey has taught me to listen to my body with every cell of my being. Turning inward with curiosity and wonder enables me to find the secret places that lie in the depths of me. This presence is like having a conversation with your body but without words.

Let me try to explain. I remember one treatment where I not only found the courage to take a plunge into the darkness, but also remained there long enough to really feel what was occupying the darkness. I became aware of a black sticky gloop, almost like tar, that occupied the whole right side of my face, jaw and head. It seemed to originate from the roof of my mouth where a tumour had been removed when I was 22.

It had all started during the summer between my 3rd and 4th year at university studying physiotherapy. I had just returned home from India after completing an elective placement working there for 9 weeks in a leprosy hospital in the southern state of Tamil Nadu. While I was there, I had become aware of a small lump in the roof of my mouth which my tongue always seemed to find. On returning home, I definitely felt it was getting bigger, so I booked an appointment with my dentist.

As soon as he saw it, he referred me to the School of Dentistry at the Royal Victoria Hospital in Belfast. He did not alarm me as he said it was probably something to do with my wisdom teeth coming through and he thought I would need all four wisdom teeth out. The appointment came quickly and I sat in the dentist's chair, the consultant took one look and said he wanted to operate the very next day.

The surgery was brutal, as all four wisdom teeth were removed, but that was the easy part - the tumour was much more extensive than they had originally thought, extending up into my sinus area. They had to take a skin flap with the blood supply and the nerve still connected from just behind my top teeth on the hard palate and swing it back over the hole on the soft palate at the right-hand side of my mouth to cover the opening left by the removal of the tumour.

You can imagine the pain and discomfort of both these areas healing, never mind the pain from the wisdom teeth being removed as well. I lived on pureed food and ice cream for weeks following the surgery.

Having missed almost 10 weeks from my final year at university, I thought I was going to have to take a year out. But my university lecturers encouraged and supported me and I managed to graduate with an honours degree in physiotherapy at the end of that year.

I will never forget the 6-week wait as the tumour was investigated. I had been shocked at just how quickly they moved to operate, so I knew it was fairly serious and could be potentially life-changing. Peter stayed by my side the whole way through, even though he absolutely hated hospitals and would wretch as he watched me being sick following the surgery.

The results came back: it was precancerous. This meant there were signs of change in some of the cells at the very centre of the tumour. They would keep a close eye on me for the next 5 years with an MRI scan every year to make sure there was no further growth. Thankfully, no further treatment was required. I vividly remember the consultant telling me if I ever got a lump or bump anywhere in my body to get it checked out immediately as it had the potential to become cancerous.

Rightly or wrongly, those words have hung over me ever since. They fertilised the growth of that dark gloop through my body. At times, I could even feel it dripping down my right arm and into my fingers as it grew and consumed my fascia. I now know this black tar is called fear.

None of us are exempt from holding on to those difficult emotions that we don't know how to deal with, so instead, we shove them below our consciousness allowing them to fester and grow.

I was learning to be present with the darkness inside, listening to what it is trying to teach me. Only by sitting here can something amazing happen, if we choose to no longer ignore our pain or try to hide it by building a mounting resistance to what is trying to surface. Instead, if we choose to journey into our hidden depths, we create more spaciousness inside of ourselves, out of which we can love more deeply, dream even bigger and live more fully, as we find the path of our purpose. In learning to let go, we create space for better things to come into our lives. In fact, it's often the most neglected parts of ourselves that when tended, can cultivate and grow the most magnificent fruits. The busyness of every day causes us to go through life distracted or avoidant, resulting in us being absent from our own existence. It stunts our growth and creativity, hindering us from receiving all that life has to offer, or all the Divine wants to express through us.

I thought I was familiar with my body. After all, I had lived with it for almost 50 years. But I was yet to discover its many hidden depths and the multitude of baggage I had chosen to carry. By accepting this invitation to find the mystery and wonder inside my very own body, it has revealed so much more than I could ever have imagined. By honouring all that lay hidden in my very depths, I have developed a new sense of wonder and awe that keeps me dedicated to continue this daily practice of sacred presence with all that lies beneath my skin.

The knowledge of every detail of our own inner landscape will only be developed with our commitment to staying put and slowly, patiently exploring our inner depths, right down to the very marrow of our bones.

STUMBLING BLOCKS

When my dad left, my world as I knew it came tumbling down around me. I had lost the security that came with my family unit. Life felt unfathomable. As well as losing my dad, we also lost our family home, having to move out of our beautiful seven-bedroom house into a caravan for a year while trying to work out what came next. I struggled! It was an incredibly difficult time. I felt alone and abandoned. My sister was soon to leave for University in Scotland and my mum withdrew into the shell that was now her existence. I felt like I had lost control, lost love and lost security. I quickly learned how to put up defences around what was left of my life, desperately trying to defend myself from any further devastation, keeping others at arm's length felt safer than risking their love leaving too.

It has taken years of healing, but now I know that even though my dad's actions were the reason for my heartache, I realise that I have to be accountable for my own reactions and choices on how to heal. Healing my heart is up to me. Nobody else can glue me back together. It's up to me to fix my broken pieces. Mending our painful wounds requires us to lean in, despite the pain.

This healing has required a conscious decision to dive deep into the pain, rather than continuing to push it deeper into the abyss of my body. We all carry heavy baggage through life that needs to be unpacked and released before we can become more whole. I am trying to navigate each emotional entanglement with more grace for myself and those around me.

As I began this healing journey, the walls of armour that I had built around myself began to drop away, melting into a pile of rubble at my feet. These mounds of melted armour still can, however, cause me to stumble. They exist on my path as stumbling blocks or hurdles, causing me to trip and distract me from my purpose.

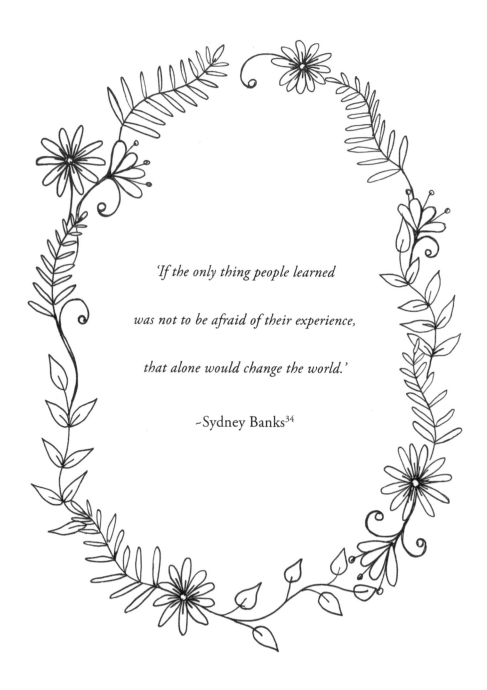

'If the only thing people learned

was not to be afraid of their experience,

that alone would change the world.'

~Sydney Banks[34]

Recently, my mentor Deb helped me to go deeper and to identify three of my biggest stumbling blocks in life:

1. Fear

2. Rejection

3. Criticism

Deb then facilitated me with a meditation that took me to stand before each in turn. Asking each stumbling block 3 questions. Let me try to explain:

Standing face to face with Fear, I ask it, 'What do you want me to know?'

Fear answered, 'I am keeping you quiet, silencing your voice. I am pulling you back from fulfilling your purpose.'

Then I asked Fear, 'When you came into being in my life, what was your purpose?'

Fear answered, 'Originally I was trying to keep you safe.'

I responded to thank Fear for its service, but then explained I no longer needed to be kept safe. I am a big girl now, I can look after myself.

Lastly, I asked Fear, 'If you could do anything in the world, what would you want to do?'

Fear responded, 'To push you forward into your purpose and make you realise that you need to find your voice and speak/write your truth.'

I did the same with Rejection, 'What do you want me to know?'

Rejection answered, 'Even though your dad rejected you, you have survived! You are worthy of love.'

What was your purpose?

'To make you strong and able to stand on your own two feet.'

If you could do anything, what would you do?

'I would help you to reject the negative voices in your head and instead listen to the wisdom of your heart.'

And lastly, I did the same with Criticism.

What do you want me to know?

'You can listen to criticism but you don't have to agree with it or take it to heart.'

What was your purpose?

'To show you that it's ok for each person to have a difference in opinion, we don't all have to share the same beliefs. Everything belongs.'

If you could do anything, what would you do?

'I would help to refine and purify and bring clarity to your words as you write. Making your book even more powerful.'

Could it be that each of our stumbling blocks or emotions that we don't like to even admit we have are each trying to actually teach us something positive?

There are so many emotions that we don't like and that we spend years ignoring or denying. But maybe it's time to listen to their truths and to really start to look at them through a different lens. Are they actually stumbling blocks or could it be that they are springboards, launching us further into life? What can they teach us? What truths lie inside?

Could it be that Anger is trying to teach us how to protect ourselves, perhaps showing us where we might need boundaries? Anger might just be trying to get our attention to show us it's ok to disagree with the status quo. Anger might help us to be heard or show us when something isn't quite right, bringing discernment.

Could Disappointment be trying to show us that there is something more meaningful in our life that we are missing out on? Disappointment might just guide us towards what it is that we really want, inviting us to create something that we long for.

Could Restlessness be showing us what or whom we want to live our life in service of? Helping to reveal to us our divine purpose? Showing us that rest and dropping inside is essential to find meaningful direction in life?

Could Impatience help us to take a fresh look at our life before we get too comfortable? Drawing us to new depths to reveal what we haven't yet discovered? Bringing us to a frontier of new possibilities? It's ok to pause - it's here that new layers can be added to create something even more beautiful.

Could it be that Shame is showing us what it's like when we stop listening to our heart's wisdom? Making us realise that our judging of others does not make us feel any better?

Could Grief show us what it is we really value, as it prepares us for new growth? Even as our tears flow we can become new again. Our grief shapes us uniquely - it's necessary to fully feel it.

It's ok to feel all of these emotions, to feel the ache deep inside. As long as you never abandon yourself - for that's how we lose who we really are.

Remembering instead that each one of these shadow parts of ourselves can reveal a pearl of hidden wisdom, they can even teach us our greatest lessons in life. So it's time to stop holding the parts of yourself that you don't like to acknowledge out of reach. Instead, learn how to embrace all of yourself, so that you can begin to grow into something beautiful.

I've learned that both forgiveness and healing are never linear. Sometimes it's two steps forward and one step back. It always helps to learn more self-compassion and self-love along the way as we journey one step at a time. I had to learn that I can't control others' choices or stop them from hurting me. Accepting this might just help me to leap over my hurdles and continue my journey with integrity and intention.

Sometimes we have to rebuild our foundations from the ground up - by listening to our hearts' wisdom, making ourselves stronger in the process, inching ever closer towards completion of our purpose here on Earth.

Don't you love when sometimes you catch glimpses of how the Universe throws something into your day at exactly the right time? The synchronicity is undeniable, and you feel like someone's got your back. Well, just that happened the very next day after I had written these words on the previous two pages, I opened a book by Tanya Markul and out jumped these beautiful words:

'Rejection taught her to let go of what didn't want her.

Abandonment showed her how to stand on her own two feet.

Betrayal awoke her intuition.

Pain broke her heart wide open.

Loneliness gave her permission to befriend herself.'

Tanya Markul[35]

Now I know that the things that wound us can actually illuminate our path.

UNMASKING FEAR

A natural reaction, when faced with emotions we don't understand or don't like the feeling of, is to shove them down and ignore them. It's only now that I'm beginning to grasp the importance of reframing my perspective and choosing to turn towards them rather than running away.

There is something very powerful when we have the courage to face our wounds, our fears and our stumbling blocks. Instead of wishing our wounds away, can we get our head around the possibility that they might just offer a resolution? That they can have a purpose? They might have something they want us to hear, if only we can soften our resistance and ask, 'what do you want to say to me?'

Fear might just tell us, 'you are alive, there is a life inside you longing to be lived more fully. The more you live your life loving what you do, the

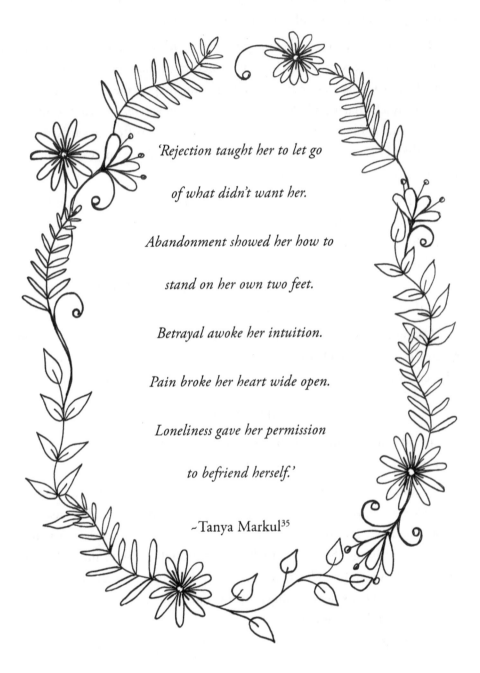

'Rejection taught her to let go

of what didn't want her.

Abandonment showed her how to

stand on her own two feet.

Betrayal awoke her intuition.

Pain broke her heart wide open.

Loneliness gave her permission

to befriend herself.'

~Tanya Markul[35]

more I will loosen my grip on you. The more you move into alignment with your purpose, the less I will need to hold you tight.'

We need to face these feelings that arise within us and even consider them as messengers of love. This was something totally new to me, but it opened up a whole new way of thinking and helped me to accept those parts of myself that I had always thought of as negative. I started to know them as truth. Emotions can be released when we soften towards them, rather than brace against them, which is what I had done for years. I simply didn't know there was a different way.

So, I started to breathe myself open and become more fluid and soft, learning to release the restrictions that hinder the healthy flow of life that flows through my body. I have now befriended those dark spaces within, that felt tight and closed. Letting them soften, and realising I can let go, rather than hold onto all that heavy baggage. Allowing them to expand and speak if they need to, as I shift from defensiveness to acceptance.

Asking my wounds to speak is the key that will open doors to finding greater peace, as I inch towards my purpose. I decide to replace my fear with curiosity, knowing I can make something sweet from something bitter.

SHADOWS

We are all human and shit happens, no matter how much we think we are unscathed by life. We all have darkness and light inside of us.

It has taken me time, but time has given me the gift of understanding that if we are brave enough to look inwards, we can find hidden treasures in our shadows. So often what we seek to avoid - sadness, grief, or pain - are the very things that can actually act as a catalyst for so much healing and growth. I totally understand that when these emotions are raw, it's too painful to even consider opening such a wound. But with time, the gift that lies within can become visible.

Our bodies are continually crying out for our gaze to turn inward.

'The wound is the place

where the Light enters you'

~Rumi[36]

Our soul is pleading for us to stop running and arrive. We spend so much time running from our past and from all of our difficult emotions, while at the same time choosing to numb ourselves with distractions, medications, or addictions, causing us to become anaesthetised to life itself.

Over the years, I have used various things such as food, shopping and TV to distract myself from what I really needed to face up to and address in my life.

Life calls us to touch the ache of our own wounds, for there is wisdom inside each one. If we are willing to explore our pain, there is a magic that draws us to the very edge. Here we can become more whole, we can unfold into our truest self, we learn to sing our own tune, discovering the truth of who we are becoming.

This work is never done, there are always shadows, even in the brightest of light. Our journey is always in motion, as we walk our path to becoming who we were created to be. And in this motion, we will always bump up against the resistance around us and within us.

So, instead of trying to rise above our anxiety or sadness, or push down our anger or fear, we can choose to own it instead. We can acknowledge life is complex and that it contains positive and negative; pleasure and pain; gain and loss; happiness and sadness. None of us are exempt from the negative, or what we perceive as negative. We get to change our way of thinking - that one is right and one is wrong - instead, choosing to believe that everything belongs. By not ignoring or numbing what we have perhaps labelled as negative, we have the opportunity to grow, to change and to learn an even deeper truth.

If we suppress our shadows, we allow them to fester and grow into an all-consuming darkness. Instead, we can integrate them, learning from them, rather than letting them blow out our flickering light and smother our eternal flame. By not ignoring them we break the power of darkness, so it can't take root in quiet ignorance.

Instead of running from our past and the parts of us that we don't like, we can practice turning inwards to see if we can catch a glimpse of what each wound is trying to teach us. This work is hard and requires a lot of trust in your own body, but it will be so worth it and it will help you move beyond the pain and chaos.

Feelings are never disguised. They are an honest representation of how we are doing on this journey called life. They speak our truth, even if we don't like the sound of their voice. It's time to stop ignoring the voices that arise from our wounds. Once we realise that negative doesn't mean bad, but more simply they are obstructions that we can learn to navigate around, we find our path forward. Yes, when we are open to looking inwards, we can change the way we navigate life. None of us will sail through life free from suffering, but if we choose to acknowledge how we feel and how we walk with our pain, we can learn to trust that even our shadows and our darkness can radically transform us. This is only possible when we lean into our wounds.

In order to evolve, we have to fully inhabit who we are, scars, wounds and all, allowing our hidden emotions to whisper something intelligent. But first, we must shine a light into those rejected and forgotten places within. By doing so, we get to bring each and every part of us into belonging.

By choosing not to run away from ourselves, we get to discover that there is fertile soil that lies beneath the shadows. We get to choose to plant the seeds of something special, little by little allowing our very own divine inheritance to sprout and grow into something beautiful.

WALKING THE PATH TO BELONGING

Often in life, we experience a period of what feels like being lost, before we find our way home, before we embrace the true medicine of our calling. Even after working towards healing, we sometimes stumble over our old wounds, when we find ourselves being triggered by current events. I've come to see how when something in the present echoes my experience of rejection as a teenager, I tend to lash out as that teenager would, despite

the fact that I am now in my 50s. Indeed by writing this book, I've come to recognise my core wounds from the past, or unresolved traumas that are still hidden in the darker recesses of my body. For example, when I decided to leave the church, it felt like a voluntary exile, but it somehow triggered my old wound of forced exile when I was rejected by my dad. All those feelings of loneliness and fear came bubbling back to the surface, causing me to feel alone and afraid.

But thankfully, somewhere deeper underneath those feelings of insecurity, I felt compelled to trust in the unknown and to let it carry me into a new place of belonging.

I am choosing to believe that I can still be lovable even when I'm not in agreement with everyone around me. My old go-to was always to keep the peace rather than speak my truth. I am learning I need to trust in my own voice, choosing to stand by the younger me and to release her from the unnecessary guilt and shame that was choking her and making her feel insecure. This pilgrimage has allowed me to retrieve all the lost parts of myself, becoming more whole as my wounded soul starts to heal. I feel like I am learning how to rebuild the fractured pieces, as I reclaim the abandoned parts of myself and let go of those that no longer serve me and who I am becoming.

It's easier to cling to what is familiar but if we are brave enough to step into our darkness and unmask the anger, the grief, the bitterness and the pain, if we push through the numbness we have built around our hearts, we will be rewarded as we learn to fully inhabit the darkness. It's not easy and sometimes we might feel the darkness will swallow us whole. But courage to travel deeper will help us to sever that which has been controlling us from the shadows, and we will begin to find freedom in the light.

I don't know anyone who doesn't love springtime. Bearing witness to all the budding, unfurling and new life.

But when it comes to our own lives evolving and growing, we are perhaps not so enthusiastic. This is because we know deep down that it can

'Nature is always calling us

into greater gestures of bravery.'

~Toko Pa Turner[37]

be a painful process, as we strip away all that weighs us down and prevents us from becoming better versions of ourselves. It requires surrender and it might feel like we are free falling, but it's only once we begin the journey that we can see what we've been missing all along and "fitting in" is no longer enough. Life is calling us forward and it requires us to "let go" of all that makes us feel safe for a time. It's time now to let go so we can soar higher, knowing this hardship will result in ultimate growth.

Shedding what we no longer need brings us closer to seeing and revealing who we really are. Choosing to no longer go against your own truth creates a more fertile place within you to begin to grow what really matters. Finding those places within where things have been silenced and rediscovering how to give them a voice.

DEEPER HONESTY

It's ok to feel a longing, to sit with it rather than expect it to be immediately soothed. We are so used to everything being instant in this life. At the touch of a button or the press of the enter key on our computer, we instantly get what we want. But I am learning that it's ok to be bored, it's ok to feel an emptiness of something that's missing and not rush to fill it with something else. That something else will all too quickly leave me feeling the exact same emptiness again.

It's ok to sit in the silence, to see what wants to be revealed. I guess I only know this because I was forced into the silence with nothing to do during the first Covid lockdown. I know every country was different, but here we were totally locked down from March 2020 for almost 5 months.

Initially, during this time, we found things to occupy us. We planted a vegetable garden and painted the garden shed, clearing out the rubbish that had been stored in it for years. With the help of my daughter Sophie and her boyfriend Sion, who unfortunately had to return home from New Zealand and spend lockdown with us here in Northern Ireland, we created a beautiful reading room in the shed. I then started going there every morning with my journal and a pot of vanilla jasmine green tea. There

I would sit watching the vegetables grow, as I listened to the birds and read and journaled. It was a magical little haven where I felt grounded and inspired. I can quite honestly say it was one of the most beautiful times of my life, as I started to grow something not only in my head and my heart, but also on the pages of my journal.

As I began to see my words in black and white on the page in front of me, my pen flowing from left to right along the lines. I slowly realised that the space between the lines was as important, if not more important, as it created the opportunity to explore my unknown depths. My writing was allowing me to know the sound of my own voice, it was allowing the truest parts of me to bubble to the surface, making space for a deeper honesty as I got to decide if I truly wanted to become the embodiment of my words. As Allison Fallon says in her book, *The Power of Writing It Down*, 'writing is prayer, spirituality, self-discovery, communication, therapy, connection. The invitation and impulse to write is not only an invitation and impulse to put a few words down on a page. It's an invitation to take ownership of our lives.'[38]

A hunger started to grow. A hunger to find my voice and to have the courage to speak without my voice shaking or being shut down.

As I sat there each and every morning, I longed to become the presence I was so hungry for, by listening long enough to what my longing was trying to say. I was learning to listen to its call, as it brought me deeper into my one true home. Our longing is trying to bring us closer to ourselves and closer to the Divine. Our journey from longing to belonging teaches us how to fully belong to each of our choices, each of our ideas. How to really belong to our body. How to belong to each regret, each loss. How to truly belong to our own story. And so my story started to unfold onto the pages of my journal.

Of course, we all find some moments in life that are too painful to fully belong, moments too full of sorrow. But these are the moments that have the greatest growth hidden inside. So I wrote freely, even about those painful moments in my own life, not knowing if they would ever reach the pages of this book. But in the writing, I know I have found healing and growth. Often we don't see these as opportunities for growth, until time has passed and we have healed enough to be able to revisit the pain. Only then can we grasp what those moments were trying to teach us in the first place.

During this time I have learned that choosing to make honest encounters with our longing, with our shadows, with our emptiness; will bring us closer to true belonging - belonging to the life we want to live. This kind of growth means that we have to be willing to engage with something that we would far rather avoid. It sometimes feels safer to live life with our eyes closed, but if we take the plunge and open them wide, this is exactly the thing that will bring us growth towards our wholeness.

CHAPTER ELEVEN

We Are Made Of Story

We are all made of story. Layer upon layer of it. Carrying wisdom deep inside the very fibres of our being.

I hope that you can now see that the fascia in our bodies is our very own connective network, mapping out our own individual stories.

It is also a transport system bringing life, nutrition and intelligence to every cell in our bodies. Perhaps it is the space between these liquid light-filled fibres (the ground substance), that is filled with memories and possibilities. As we trace a path across our wounds, it shows us our journey through life. Every little thing we experience in life is transmitted and held somewhere in our body. Some experiences cause deep gaping craters, while others can cause a few puckers here and there.

It's our job to not ignore, but to hunt out these wrinkles and wounds. To recognise it's all part of our lives storied within, the elaborate embroidery of our internal landscape showing us the way home.

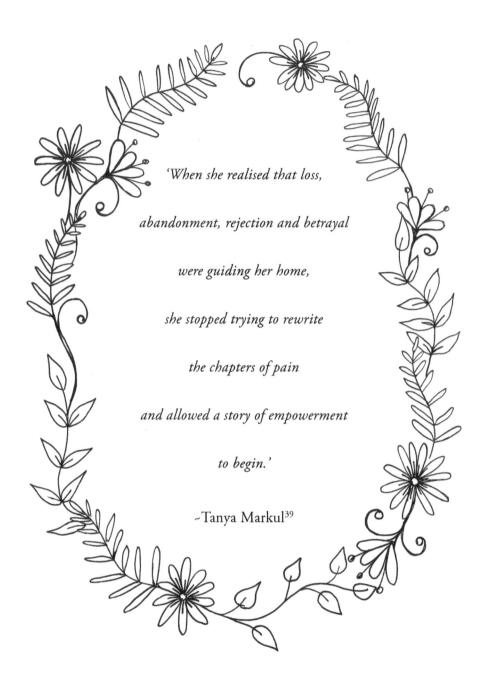

'When she realised that loss,

abandonment, rejection and betrayal

were guiding her home,

she stopped trying to rewrite

the chapters of pain

and allowed a story of empowerment

to begin.'

~Tanya Markul[39]

Our history is embedded fathoms deep inside. Each memory contained within its very own curves and lines, casting shadows of light and darkness, we each have our very own pattern, original to us.

We have endless possibilities to unfurl our own unique purpose.

Looking inward allows us to see the mystery, to feel its rhythms arise, awakening deep within our bones, calling us forward on this path of life, choosing to bring beauty and richness, as we seek out our own individual creativity with a newfound awakening and awareness that comes out of exploring and honouring deep inside our very being.

I am now understanding how my traumas have become metabolised in my very cells. I feel I am beginning to see how my flaws have value, acting as medicine for my brokenness. I am allowing my gifts to grow out of my wounds, as my story unfolds.

We all have a biological necessity to tell our story. Storytelling is part of who we are. It has been evident from the beginning of time. Even our dreams help our body to process a narrative.

I want to ask you what's in your web of intricately woven fibres? Perhaps writing down your story or journaling will help you to create a kind of wholeness.

It is my dream that by writing my story, which goes from chaos to pattern, I might help someone to find their own beautiful tapestry in life.

As I began this writing journey, I did so with a longing to belong. I dropped into the unknown and managed to find a life full of stories, woven together in a shimmering web of complex entanglements.

I have discovered that we can break open these old stories and regrow them, that we don't have to remain captive to them. Each story is deeply encoded in the memory of our bodies. The landscapes which hold our stories can change as we shift what lies at the heart of these old stories we have been telling ourselves. This shift will show us how to become exactly who we were created to be. The threads of each story remain, so we can take up these threads and use them to weave a new way of being in the world. We are the weaver, the one who can weave our threads into meaning and pattern if we choose.

We have created those threads out of our very substance, out of our own hearts. Perhaps it's time to gather some new threads, time to strengthen the ragged edges of our own being and then weave ourselves back into the fabric of belonging. Discovering that we are rooted and that we are made to rise, to become deeply enmeshed in the web of life.

Healing is not a journey that takes place in our heads. It's a journey that takes us out of our heads and weaves us back into the shimmering web of our fascial system as we all become interwoven into the web of the universe.

Turns out my life's purpose isn't supposed to be small, silent and accommodating. It was all about finding my voice and speaking my truth through telling my story.

Believe in yourself.

You have the power to create a new story.

Begin with small steps out of your comfort zone.

Stay open to new possibilities.

And enjoy this journey of becoming.

'As I journey through this life,

I am continually enriched by the gifts of discovery

as I evolve to find new freedom of thought, with the

integrity of my mind, body and soul.'

Notes

INTRODUCTION

(1) Lopez, B. (2013). Sliver of Sky. Harpers Magazine

(2) O'Donohue, J. Unfinished Poem. Retrieved May, 2021 <goodreads.com/quotes/121160-unfinished-poem-i-would-love-to-live-like-a-river>

(3) Holden, R (2020). Spiritual Resilience Mastermind Programme.

CHAPTER ONE

(4) Blackie, S. (2018). The Enchanted Life: Unlocking The Magic of The Everyday. September Publishing

CHAPTER THREE

(5) Bridge, M. Retrieved May 2021, <quotes.net/quote/42444>

(6) Blackie, S. (2018). The Enchanted Life: Unlocking The Magic of The Everyday. September Publishing

(7) Swart, T. (2019). The Source: Open Your Mind, Change Your Life. Vermilion.

(8) One of John's phrases often used when teaching

(9) Olanubi, D. Retrieved May 2021, <goodreads.com/quotes/1136182-i-wish-to-live-a-life-that-causes-my-soul/>

(10) von Goethe, J, W. Retrieved May 2021, <forbes.com/quotes/5037/>

(11) Buddha., Kornfield, J. (1996). Buddha's Little Instruction Book. Rider

CHAPTER FOUR

(12) Lipton, B. (2015). The Biology of Belief: Unleashing the Power of Consciousness, Matter & Miracles. Hay House UK

(13)Brown, B. (2013). Daring Greatly: How the Courage to Be Vulnerable Transforms the Way We Live, Love, Parent and Lead. Penguin UK

(14) definition of *Interoception*: the awareness of what is going on in your own body, so that you can identify any residual unnecessary tension from unconscious habitual holding and bracing patterns

(15) Chopra, D. Retrieved May 2021, <azquotes.com/quote/551421>

(16) Gandhi, M. Retrieved May 2021, <goodreads.com/quotes/760902-we-but-mirror-the-world-all-the-tendencies-present-in>

(17) Huxley, A. (2005). Island. Vintage Classics

CHAPTER FIVE

(18) Dobson, K. (2017). Bitten by a Camel: Leaving Church, Finding God. Fortress Press

(19) Jung, C. Retrieved May 2021, <brainyquote.com/quotes/carl_jung_714938/>

(20) Markul, T. (2019). The She Book. Andrews McMeel Publishing

(21) Rumi. Retrieved May 2021, <poemhunter.com/poem/the-breeze-at-dawn/>

CHAPTER SIX

(22) Ruiz Jr, D, M. (2014). The Five Levels of Attachment: Toltec Wisdom for the Modern World. Hay House

(23) Campbell, J. (1989). The Power of Myth. Bantam Doubleday Dell Publishing Group

(24) Yuknavitych, L. (2019). The Chronology of Water. Canongate Books

CHAPTER SEVEN

(25) Brown, B. (2015). Rising Strong. Vermillion

(26) Blackie, S. (2016). If Women Rose Rooted: A Life-changing Journey to Authenticity and Belonging. September Publishing

(27) Nin, A. Poem: Risk. Retrieved May 2021 <famouspoetsandpoems. com/poets/anais_nin/poems/3313>

(28) Turner, T. (2017). Belonging: Remembering Ourselves Home. Her Own Room Press

CHAPTER EIGHT

(29) Turner, T. (2017). Belonging: Remembering Ourselves Home. Her Own Room Press

(30) Pueblo, Y. (2019). 18 April. Available at: <twitter.com/yungpueblo/status/1118682962227290112?lang=en/> (Accessed: 7th May, 2021)

CHAPTER NINE

(31) Turner, T. (2017). Belonging: Remembering Ourselves Home. Her Own Room Press

CHAPTER TEN

(32) Voskamp, A. (2016). 3 October. Available at: <twitter.com/annvoskamp/status/782941512061575168?lang=en> (Accessed: 7th May, 2021)

(33) Cousineau, P. Campbell, J. (1999). The Hero's Journey: Joseph Campbell on His Life and Work. Element Books Ltd

(34) Banks, S. Retrieved May 2021 <azquotes.com/quote/84595/>

(35) Markul, T. (2019). The She Book. Andrews McMeel Publishing

(36) Rumi. Retrieved May 2021 <goodreads.com/quotes/103315-the-wound-is-the-place-where-the-light-enters-you/>

(37) Turner, T. (2017). Belonging: Remembering Ourselves Home. Her Own Room Press

(38) Fallon, A. (2021). The Power of Writing It Down: A Simple Habit to Unlock Your Brain and Reimagine Your Life. Zondervan Books

CHAPTER ELEVEN

(39) Markul, T. (2019). The She Book. Andrews McMeel Publishing

Acknowledgements

Firstly, I want to thank my husband of 30 years for his steadfast love, encouragement and support, both in my many trips to America for training and in writing this book.

Thank you Peter for believing in me. I love you.

Thank you to my children, Jacob and Sophie, who have cheered me on from the sidelines. I am incredibly proud of you both.

Mum - I will forever be grateful for your love, sacrifice and encouragement.

Words cannot express how much John F. Barnes has impacted, transformed and altered the trajectory of my life. Thank you John for your persistence and courage to keep teaching what is true and authentic healing work. For sharing your gift with so many. Your instinctive knowledge is something we all dream of. You have given me a greater sense of meaning and belonging in the world.

A special thanks to Sophie and Lara for taking my written words and bringing them into form, in this book you now hold in your hands. Thank you Sophie for setting up the website www.findingmysterywithin.com and Lara Czornyj for all the beautiful artwork, edits and for bringing it all together. Much love to you both.

Thank you Mary Flora Hart, (my niece) for the beautiful picture you created of my past, present and future selves.

Thanks to Deb and our little circle of seven women who have met faithfully over the last year. For your guidance, encouragement and inspiration which has helped each of us create what was on our hearts. Without each of you, this book would not have come into form.

Thank you to everyone who took time out of their busy schedules to read this book before it was published. Thanks for your encouragement, support and guidance.

Thanks to you, the reader, I hope you have been inspired to take those first tentative steps on your own healing journey.

About The Author

Julie McCammon is a physiotherapist and expert level practitioner of the John F. Barnes approach to Myofascial Release (MFR). She is currently based in Northern Ireland and runs her own private practice and holistic healing space, The Garden Room. Here, she assists her clients in their quest to resolve pain and optimise their health.

Her first book *Finding Mystery Within* is a self-published memoir which evolved from over three decades of a career in healing, and the journey it took her on in re-discovering the self-worth she lost as a child. She beautifully blends her own unique experiences with an intimate grasp of bodywork and invites us to transform our pain into passion.

Julie is a wife and mother of two adult children, and continues to support them and others in their pursuits of self-discovery, authenticity and growth. You can keep up to date with her work on Instagram and Facebook.

Made in United States
Troutdale, OR
07/10/2023

11110153R00126